D1615760

MUSIC 109

MUSIC 109

Notes on Experimental Music

FOREWORD BY ROBERT ASHLEY

Wesleyan University Press
Middletown, Connecticut

WESLEYAN UNIVERSITY PRESS
Middletown CT 06459
www.wesleyan.edu/wespress

Manufactured in the United States of America
Designed by Eric M. Brooks
Typeset in Whitman and Calluna Sans
by Passumpsic Publishing

Wesleyan University Press is a member of the Green Press Initiative. The paper used in this book meets their minimum requirement for recycled paper.

Library of Congress
Cataloging-in-Publication Data
Lucier, Alvin.
Music 109: notes on experimental music /
Alvin Lucier; foreword by Robert Ashley.
pages cm
Includes index.
ISBN 978-0-8195-7297-4 (cloth: alk. paper)—
ISBN 978-0-8195-7298-1 (ebook)
1. Lucier, Alvin. 2. Avant-garde (Music)
I. Title.
ML410.L8973A3 2012
780.92—dc23 2012008721

5 4 3 2 1

Again for

WENDY & AMANDA

And for

SUSAN & SUE-ELLEN

CONTENTS

FOREWORD

Music 109 is a thorough, modern history of a particular group of composers and their work. This history begins in the 1950s and ends roughly in the 1980s. In colleges and universities where the history of contemporary music is part of the curriculum, this book will solve many teachers' problems about what ideas, what composers, and what compositions are important to understand from that history. What Alvin Lucier presents so clearly here, with quotations from scores, will make a classroom discussion of those ideas easy.

We are in the time of what young composers now speak of as the music that has influenced their ideas. The study begins *after* the time of Harry Partch, Conlin Nancarrow, Henry Cowell, and Virgil Thompson. But even with its attention solely to the music of the past fifty years, it takes us to composers and compositions that for many younger musicians are almost legendary—compositions that everybody has heard, or heard about, but that in most cases have not been studied.

As we read, we discover that many of these compositions and the ideas under discussion have not previously been understood as coming from a common purpose or shared idea. In this way, the book is a serious academic history, but Lucier relates these ideas to us in the form of stories, talking to us as he talked to his students. He is never ironic about what he is doing. His enthusiasm is clear and warm hearted; this music means something to him.

Many of the compositions discussed here, and the ideas they represent, remind me of times I have spent with Alvin. I read the title *Chambers* and I am in Scandinavia, probably at the Sonja Henie museum in Oslo. There are eight of us on this tour. When it comes time to play *Chambers* everybody takes some sort of "chamber" out of the suitcase that Alvin has brought—small, covered pots and jars, tea kettles, tin cans, and, finally, four or five conch shells (in the days before conch shells were available from the instrument-rental shop). Everybody walks around the performance space presenting sounds to the audience. Then everybody—one by one and very slowly—walks through the doors of the concert hall into a garden that adjoins the hall and disappears into the darkness outside. The concert has ended in a kind of magic.

Then I am in a New England–style house across the street from the Wesleyan campus. Alvin is attached to a mysterious device through wires patched to his head. I don't know what he is going to do. He closes his eyes and appears to be concentrating fiercely on something. A few seconds later there are sounds coming from one of the other rooms in the house. They are percussion sounds. But even now, decades later, I remember vividly that I thought the sounds were of distant thunder. I had never heard that sound in music. I was enchanted.

Then, at the Rose Art Museum. Alvin has invited David Behrman, Gordon Mumma, and me to give a concert there. (Maybe this was the occasion when, after the concert, we were having a drink at Alvin's house, and it occurred to Alvin and me to invent the Sound Arts Union. We went into the other room to check the idea with David and Gordon. They approved.) For the concert Alvin performs *Wolfman*, a recent composition of mine. In just a few years I came to realize that Alvin was the only person ever to perform the piece correctly.

Finally, for this account, one story of the numberless times we spent together: Alvin comes to Ann Arbor as a guest of the ONCE Festival. Four performers are preparing to use his Sondols (devices that give off powerful clicking sounds that bounce off the various physical objects in the space and, when the performer gives attention to the clicks, help the performer negotiate the space). The lights go down. The performance starts. The gallery is filled with loud clicks bouncing off everything. This is an amazing sound. Nobody in the audience has had this experience of sound.

Alvin is characteristically modest in *Music 109* about his major contribution to this half-century of music in which the language changed so radically. In fact, he is modest about the change itself—as if this sort of thing happens all the time. This book makes the work of a couple of dozen composers—the pioneers in the world of sound-as-more-important-(for the moment)-than-what-the-composer-does-with-the-sound—simple, finally, to understand. And these are the composers and the compositions important to listen to—in order to understand.

Robert Ashley

MUSIC 109

1

SYMPHONY

Symphony No. 4

When I went to college we studied the masterpieces of European music. If you wanted to be a professional composer, you would go to Europe after college to finish up your musical education. Before World War I many American composers went to Munich to study with an organist named Josef Rheinberger; after the war they went to Paris to study with Nadia Boulanger. Walter Piston and Aaron Copland studied with her. My three composition teachers in graduate school studied with her. The entire batch of American students was nicknamed the "Boulangerie." That's French for bakery. Anyway, one felt that one's spiritual home was in Europe. We all thought that American classical music wasn't as good as European music. And for good reasons. It's hard to compete with Bach, Beethoven, and Brahms, not to mention such modern masters as Bartok, Schoenberg, and Stravinsky. We all had inferiority complexes. There was no concept of World Music then. And even though we all loved jazz, there were no courses devoted to it. We simply played it outside of school. It's very different now, but when I was in college that was true.

Charles Ives graduated from Yale in 1898. He studied composition with Horatio Parker, who, by the way, had studied with Rheinberger. When Ives left Yale he knew he couldn't make a living as a composer, so he went into the insurance business. The firm of Ives and Myrick became one of the most successful insurance companies in New York. He wrote music at night, knowing that much of his work would never be played, at least in his lifetime. When Ives retired because of ill health, he was a wealthy man, but he only took enough money out of his company to live in reasonable comfort.

Throughout his creative life, Ives wrote startlingly original works using polychords, polyrhythms, quartertones, and other innovative devices he learned from his father, a band conductor and indefatigable music experimenter. His *Symphony No. 4* (written between 1910 and 1916 but not performed until 1965, by Leopold Stokowski) requires three conductors to manage separate instrumental groups playing in different meters and tempos. In the first movement, a distant chamber orchestra, consisting of harp and solo strings, usually situated in the balcony, plays heavenly music against the heavy, symphonic music of the main orchestra. (As a child Ives had watched a parade in Danbury during which two bands marched from opposite ends of the street, playing in different keys and tempos.) This movement is only about three minutes long. It's marked *maestoso*. That's Italian for majestic or stately.

Throughout the history of music there have been examples of instrumental and vocal groups playing separately. Giovanni Gabrieli (1555–1612) composed works for multiple choirs in Saint Mark's Cathedral in Venice. There's a ballroom scene in Mozart's *Don Giovanni* where three small orchestras on stage play different musics in different tempos simultaneously, $\frac{3}{4}$, $\frac{2}{4}$, and $\frac{3}{8}$. In Gabrieli, the spatially separated musics form part of a whole; they go together. In the Mozart they more or less fit together, but every once in a while they split apart rhythmically. Mozart could get away with that in 1787 because it served the theatrical purpose of providing different musics for different social classes—a minuet for the aristocracy, a contradance for the peasants. But in Ives the musics are completely separate: one group is playing one kind of music, another group, another kind. It was astonishing, that idea. One would think you couldn't hear two musics at the same time, but the contrary seems to be true. The more differentiated they are, the more clearly you can hear them. The work is filled with quotations, too. In the second movement you can hear *Marching Through Georgia*, *In the Sweet Bye and Bye*, *Turkey in the Straw*, *Yankee Doodle*, and (Ives's favorite) *Columbia the Gem of the Ocean*.

One of my composition teachers at Yale thought that Ives wrote music with one eye closed. He meant that Ives didn't take enough care with the details of notation. Aaron Copland, too, thought that the "weakness" in Ives's music was due to a lack of self-criticism from not hearing his music played enough. Even John Cage criticized Ives for using patriotic songs instead of sources from around the world. None of these men gives credit to Ives's great innovations and high aspirations for music as a philosophical endeavor. Ives titled the four movements of his *Concord Sonata*, which he composed between 1911 and 1915, after the New England Transcendentalists *Emerson*, *Hawthorne*, *The Alcotts*, and *Thoreau*. His *Essays before a Sonata* presents his impression of the spirit of Transcendentalism and puts forth his own philosophical and musical ideas. The *Essays* is filled with amazing statements: "Debussy's content would have been worthier if he had hoed corn or sold newspapers for a living," for example. The ideas contained in Emerson's famous essay, *Self-Reliance*, plus a quote from *The American Scholar*, "We have listened too long to the courtly muses of Europe," characterize Ives's thinking.

A group of students and I went down to Alice Tully Hall in New York City to hear the American premiere of Elliott Carter's *Fifth String Quartet* (1995). Each instrument had a very pronounced personality, different from the others, like characters in a play. Each voice even had a different set of intervals that identified it and its instrument. It was amazing how clearly one could hear each instrument, as it played along with almost complete independence. The viola part was particularly vivid. It reminded me of Ives's *String Quartet No. 2* (1907–1913), in which the second violinist, whom Ives named "Rollo," plays music distinctly different from the others. He's the most conservative of the four. Throughout the second movement, *Arguments: Allegro con spirito*, he tries to establish order, playing steady rhythms. Every so often, he continues blissfully along by himself. As a young man, Elliott Carter had cultivated a friendship with Ives. One of the criticisms of Carter's music is that it's too complicated to hear; you can't tell what's going on. But it's in late nineteenth-century symphonic music, where all the instruments are blended into a whole, that the individual parts are difficult to discern.

2

STUDIO FONOLOGICO

Music Walk with Dancers

In 1960 I was awarded a Fulbright Fellowship to study music in Italy. I spent the first summer in Venice, followed by two years in Rome. I was lucky to have a scholarship. I remember going to a concert at La Fenice (The Phoenix) theater in Venice. It was a beautiful little late eighteenth-century Italian opera house. Verdi's *Rigoletto* had its first performance there. I had seen advertised a concert of composer John Cage, pianist David Tudor, and dancers Merce Cunningham and Carolyn Brown. I decided to go. The concert began with David Tudor walking down the aisle of the theater and diving under the piano, making sounds on the underside of the instrument. The audience screamed. At the same time Cage, Cunningham, and Brown walked around the theater reading cards with instructions as to actions they could make. They used the whole theater as a performance space. I think the piece was *Music Walk with Dancers*. At one point, Cage rose up from below the stage on a hydraulic platform playing the piano. People were furious. I was flabbergasted. He used a radio as one of his instruments, too. At one moment he turned it on and got the voice of the pope asking for peace in the world. It was a wonderful moment. One man strode down the aisle with a cane. He hit the piano and said, "Now I am a composer!" I guess you could say that concert blew my mind. I stopped writing music for a year.

Scambi

In the early Sixties, there were several electronic music studios in Europe. Pierre Schaeffer had established a *musique concrète* studio in Paris. *Musique concrète* is music made from recorded natural and man-made sounds. A famous work from that period, by Pierre Henry, a collaborator of Schaeffer's, was called *Variations for a Door and a Sigh*. The source material for this work consisted entirely of the two sounds in the title. German composers Karlheinz Stockhausen and Herbert Eimert founded a studio at the West German Radio in Cologne, and Italian composers Luciano Berio and Bruno Maderna founded the Studio di Fonologia in Milan. The Milan studio consisted of a bank of twelve audio oscillators (guess why?), a white noise generator, an echo chamber, a few modification devices, including a ring modulator, filters of one kind or another, a few tape machines, and some accessory equipment. Do you know what white noise is? Theoretically, it's all frequencies randomly mixed together, producing a hissing sound. It's a valuable tool in testing electronic circuits and acoustic spaces because it's neutral and covers a wide frequency band. If you want to discover the acoustical signature of a space you can pump in bursts of white noise. A spectrum analyzer will show you where the resonances are. White noise was a wonderful sound source for composers because it had a rich timbre. You could filter out frequency bands, too, giving it the suggestion of pitch. White noise is to sound what color is to light.

In these early electronic music studios you basically worked with reel-to-reel tape recorders. There were no cassette or digital tape recorders then. The machines ran at various speeds: the faster, the better the sound quality. The professional standard at that time was 15 inches per second (ips), so if you cut one inch of tape, you got one-fifteenth of a second of sound. If you slowed the machine down to 7½ ips, you not only slowed the sounds down by half, but lowered their pitch by one octave, too. Playing the tape backward produced interesting results because the natural decay of a sound now became a gradual attack; the end of the sound would be abrupt. A composer could accomplish a great deal by simply manipulating tape. He or she could modify sounds, too, by adding reverberation and filtering. Bandpass filters enabled you to choose certain regions of a wideband sound complex; ring modulators added and subtracted two frequencies fed into it, producing raucous sidebands. Reverb, of course, gave everything a spacy sound, which good composers used judiciously. One of the techniques in the Milan studio was to record a library of sounds by mixing several sources—chords of oscillator tones, ring modulated sound complexes, strands of reverberated white noise—then hang the tapes up on the wall, marking each one so you'd know what was on it.

The Fulbright office in Rome got me permission to work there for two weeks in 1961. I was anxious to explore the new medium. My mind was a blank, which was wonderful because I could let everything just come in. There was a library of all the tape pieces composed by visiting composers. I listened to them all. One was a short work composed by Belgian composer Henri Pousseur. It was called *Scambi* (1958). That's Italian for "exchanges." The sound material for *Scambi* is colored noise—white noise filtered in such a way as to give it pitch. There are two very different types of material: one, extremely short bursts of sound, heard as single events and in longer trains (you can imagine how many splices it takes to make a four- or five-second group); the other, longer and more continuous strands, which swoop and undulate. This can be accomplished by manually varying the speed of the recorder, slowing it down and speeding it up, or shifting the regions of filtering. From time to time the material is colored by reverberation. The work consists of sixteen sequences of different lengths that may be interchanged in an almost infinite number of ways. Pousseur himself made several versions of the piece. So did his friend Berio. Because each section may be juxtaposed with any other, there can be no obvious climaxes or points of hierarchical importance. Instead, one hears an unending redistribution of material that may have local high points. The form is open. Pousseur realized that a fixed work on tape may be deadly and he strove to give it life.

There was much talk in those days about additive and subtractive synthesis. If you had enough sine-wave oscillators you could eventually produce white noise. Conversely, white noise, which consisted of all frequencies randomly mixed together, could be filtered down to one sine-wave tone. This was a theoretical notion, as far as I could see; I'd never heard it done in real life. But there was a lot of talk about this, as if this dichotomy could give a theoretical basis to this new medium.

Fontana Mix

One day as I was working, Marino Zuccheri, the engineer, remarked that John Cage had been there a couple of years earlier, in 1958. I thought, "Oh, no!" He said that on the day that Mr. Cage arrived, he simply sat down and proceeded to draw all the equipment in the studio, every dial, every knob, even the brand names of the components. (He had studied architecture in Paris and was a fine draftsman.) Cage explained that prehistoric people, when they were afraid of some wild animal, would draw a picture of it to get over their fear. It's a marvelous idea, whether it's true or not. After Zuccheri described all the components of the studio, Cage asked him if he had a portable tape recorder. Zuccheri said yes and agreed to meet Cage the next day. Instead of making a piece using all the fancy equipment and electronically generated sounds in the studio, Cage preferred to go outside and record some city sounds. They spent days recording animals in the zoo, machines, people on trams, all sorts of environmental sounds. He and Zuccheri brought those sounds on tape back into the studio. Cage arranged the sounds, as well as some others, into six classes, including city and country sounds, instrumental and electronic sounds, wind sounds (singing), and very quiet ones needing amplification.

Cage spent the next couple of months splicing tape. To help him decide how to assemble the material, he resorted to chance procedures. He made a "score" consisting of transparent sheets with dots, drawings of curved lines, a graph with a hundred horizontal and twenty vertical units and a sheet with a straight line. Randomly superimposing the sheets, and connecting points in the graph to those outside it, would give him readings to determine musical parameters such as frequency, timbre, duration, and loudness. I think he took sounds at random, not knowing what exactly was on each piece of tape.

What impresses one was his doggedness in splicing thousands of scraps of tape over such a long period of time. Even though the determinations were generated by chance procedures, the manual work was exact and not subject to chance at all. He called the piece *Fontana Mix*, named after the woman who owned the *pensione* he was staying at while working in Milan.

Aria

Around this time Cage composed an aria for Cathy Berberian, an American opera singer who was living in Milan. She was married to Berio at the time. Do you know what an aria is? It's a solo number in an opera. The action stops and the singer has an opportunity to sing for an extended time, usually something of an expressive nature. In provincial opera houses in Italy, it's typical for the audience to wait for the arias — the high emotional points — not paying much attention to the other parts of the opera. Do you know Casey Stengel's famous phrase, "It's not over 'til the fat lady sings"? Well, that refers to the final aria a soprano might sing at the end of an opera.

The work may be sung in whole or in any part, by a voice of any range, alone or with *Fontana Mix* or with any parts of the *Concert for Piano and Orchestra* (another of Cage's works). There are squiggly lines in eight colors, representing various singing styles, including jazz (dark blue), folk (green), Marlene Dietrich (purple), and coloratura (yellow). There are words or parts of words underneath the squiggles in several languages, including Armenian, Russian, Italian, French, and English. It's clear that *Aria* was tailor-made for Ms. Berberian. (She was Armenian-American and had studied opera.) There are also black squares that indicate noises that the performer may choose for herself. She chose foot stomps, finger snaps, tongue clicks, expressions of sexual pleasure, etc. There is no time, no meter, no notes, no rhythm. The singer is free to determine all aspects of the performance not specifically notated. For this recording the two works were simply mixed together. No attempt was made to synchronize the tapes and yet in a strange way they seem to go together. Together, *Aria* with *Fontana Mix* (1958) is one of the most shocking recorded works I know. I love to start the year with it. It sounds wonderful.

I find I listen to it differently from other music. Even though the performance is fixed on tape, the work itself is composed by indeterminate means. Therefore none of the conventional relationships you might normally hear in a musical work is present. One hears different things each time one listens to it, which isn't so much the case with music composed in a conventional manner. Because there is a lack of relationships that one remembers from previous music, one hears it differently each time. I can't prove this, but I'm sure it's true.

Once the score is fixed you don't alter it. Cage would never throw out something he didn't like on the basis of taste. Other composers have worked this way. They've used chance procedures to make material that they would otherwise not make; then they choose what they like and make the piece the way they would make it anyway. That's a half-baked way of working, don't you think? Cage doesn't use chance procedures to get interesting material that he may or may not choose to like or dislike; he simply accepts it all. Once he sets up his chance procedures, he follows them to the nth degree.

Indeterminacy gets personal preference out of the compositional process. Isn't that a shocking idea? Weren't we always taught that art was about self-expression? What have Cage's pieces to do with self-expression? Nothing. They've got everything to do with discovery. People sometimes say his work is nihilistic; they think he just throws things together. In fact he's extremely meticulous with his scores. He doesn't cheat, either. I know he doesn't because I've worked with him.

3
INDETERMINACY

Indeterminacy is a collection of ninety stories that John Cage began writing in 1958. I'd like to play some of them. It's a good way to start the year. They always make me feel good, especially when the weather gets bad. These CDs were sent to me by Leslie Spitz-Edson, a former Wesleyan student who took this class in the late Eighties. She works for the Smithsonian Institution in Washington, and recently produced the reissue of the old Cage/Tudor Folkways recording in a beautiful boxed set. I got them for free.

You'll notice that Cage reads in a special way. He tells each story at a different speed. Each one is one minute long. If the text is short, he speaks slowly. If it's long—two or three paragraphs—he speaks fast. In order to make his lectures interesting, and not dull and boring as so many lectures are, he times them and talks in a certain way. It's like music but there's no beat or meter to it. Are there any other musics on planet earth without a beat or meter? Gregorian chant, for example. The rhythm follows the words. Maybe it's a mistake to say this resembles music. Perhaps we should have simply said this is what it is. Somewhere Cage said he thought of it as poetry. Anyway, they're wonderful stories. Let's not worry about it.

He told thirty of them at the Brussels World's Fair in 1958. To have an American composer come over to Europe and tell funny stories must have been shocking. You didn't hear too many serious composers telling funny stories then. The talks and lectures on art and music you would have heard in Europe around that time would have been very serious, scientific, and analytical.

Cage's stories are filled with ideas that tell you something about his aesthetics of music. For example, there's the one about the people diving in an outdoor swimming pool and the music in the jukebox inside seems to be accompanying them, even though they couldn't be hearing it. One activity doesn't have anything to do with the other, but if they're happening at the same time, there is a relationship or perhaps a non-relationship. That led Cage to thinking how one notices many things at the same time in everyday life. You walk down the street, look at the trees, see somebody, breathe, and hear the sounds around you. You can focus on many things at once. And whereas most music we know is made to focus one on itself—you're supposed to sit in a concert hall and be attentive to some musical masterpiece—Cage sees that one can perceive many things at the same time.

Indeterminacy is about so many things. The stories are written out. The sounds that go along with the talking seem to be random and yet sometimes they punctuate what is being said. The ones that sound like a metal spring are made by a Slinky! There are a lot of piano sounds, too, and a dog barking. David Tudor used sounds from *Fontana Mix* and *Concert for Piano and Orchestra* as accompaniment. He didn't synchronize the sounds with Cage's reading. They're just in there at the same time.

Cage claimed to be an anarchist. By that he didn't mean that everyone simply does whatever they want to or does things in a shoddy manner. If everybody did whatever they did as well as they could, there wouldn't be the need to refer to a higher authority. When he was at Wesleyan in the Sixties, he taught a course in which he sent everyone to the library to find a different book. The students used chance operations to generate the call numbers. They all came back with different books on different subjects, some even in different languages. Cage thought it was a stupid idea for everybody to read the same thing. He thought it would be more interesting if everyone read something different.

I Ching

In 1951 Christian Wolff gave John Cage a copy of the *I Ching*, the ancient Chinese book of oracles. A new translation of Richard Wilhelm's German version had just been published by Princeton University Press as part of the Bollingen Series, which also contained the collected works of Carl Jung. (Bollingen is a town in Switzerland where Jung had a country house.) Christian's father, Kurt Wolff, was the publisher of the series. In the Thirties he had been a distinguished publisher in Germany. He was Kafka's first publisher. Later, in the United States, he founded Pantheon Books, which published such writers as Boris Pasternak, Gunter Grass, and Anne Morrow Lindbergh.

For much of his life Jung had consulted the oracle as a means of exploring the unconscious. In his Foreword to the *I Ching* he coins the term "synchronicity," which takes the events in space and time as meaning something more than mere chance, an interdependence of objective events among themselves, as well as with the subjective (psychic) states of the observer. It is an Eastern concept diametrically opposed to the Western one of causality. Just as causality describes a sequence of events—A causes B, which in turn causes C, and so forth—so synchronicity deals with events happening at the same time. It's what we call coincidence. Jung also says that every natural process is interfered with in some way by chance and that Western science, which is based on averages or statistics, is far too general to do justice to the variety of human experience. He cites as an example a quartz crystal, no two of which are exactly alike, although all are clearly hexagonal.

The *I Ching*, also called the *Book of Changes*, consists of sixty-four hexagrams with accompanying texts and commentaries. The ancient way of generating hexagrams was by dividing yarrow stalks. (The common yarrow, also known as milfoil, is an herbal plant valued for its curative properties. Achilles used it to heal the wounds of his soldiers and to stop their bleeding.) You chose fifty of them, then put one aside. Then you divided the remaining forty-nine into two random heaps. One stalk from the right-hand heap was put between the ring finger and little finger of the left hand. Then the left-hand heap was placed in the left hand and the right hand would take from it bundles of four, until there were four or fewer stalks remaining. The right-hand heap was counted off by fours and the remainder was placed between the middle finger and forefinger of the left hand. The sum of the stalks was either nine or five. The single stalk held between the little and ring finger was disregarded. Now you had either an eight or a four. The four was regarded as a whole unit and given the number three; the number eight was regarded as a double unit and given the value of two. This procedure continued until the numbers six, seven, eight, and nine were produced and repeated six times to form hexagrams of still and changing lines.

Another way of generating hexagrams is by throwing coins. You designate one side as a yin, with the value of two, and the reverse as a yang, with a value of three. By tossing three coins you get numbers six, seven, eight, or nine. Numbers seven and eight are positive and negative rests, respectively; six and nine, positive and negative changes. The changing lines are more important than the resting ones. Rest is merely a state of polarity that always posits movement as its complement. You throw the coins six times to get six lines, starting from the bottom up, completing the hexagram. You then look it up in the book.

Recently I threw coins and got hexagram 52, *Ken/Keeping Still, Mountain*. The image of this hexagram is a mountain, the youngest son of heaven and earth. The male principle is at the top, because it strives upward by nature; the female principle is below, since the direction of its movement is downward. The hexagram addresses the problem of achieving a quiet heart. The text suggests keeping the back, as well as the toes, calves, hips, trunk and jaws still. Possibly the words of the text embody directions for the practice of yoga, but there are metaphysical or psychological meanings in the text as well. Keeping the back at rest, for example, means forgetting the ego; keeping the jaw still helps avoid injudicious speech. A hexagram worked out in a certain moment of time is understood as an indicator of the essential situation prevailing at that moment. You read the text for wisdom and understanding, that it may spur you to action. I've decided to study yoga and stop talking so much.

Music of Changes

Cage was drawn to the *Key for Identifying the Hexagrams* at the end of the *Book of Changes*. It was a grid consisting of the eight upper trigrams across the top; the eight lower ones, down the left side. Cage was fond of charts; he had used the Magic Square in several early works. For *Music of Changes* (1951), a work in four parts for solo piano, he used the *I Ching* to generate random numbers from one to sixty-four, to construct charts that referred to certain musical parameters: superpositions (how many sounds are happening at the same time in a given structural space), durations, sounds, and dynamics. In the charts for sounds, thirty-two of them (the even numbers) are silences. In those for dynamics he uses only sixteen numbers—one, five, nine, etc. (yarrow stalks in bundles of four?). He wanted to make a composition that was free of personal taste and memory, which existed outside the traditions of music, and was, above all, free of psychology.

There are wonderful images in the *I Ching*—*Fire in the Lake*, *The Wanderer*, *Inner Truth*—but Cage didn't use them. One can understand why. He didn't want to refer in any way to psychological states, the unconscious, or superstition. When computers came into widespread use, he started using them to generate hexagrams. When he was here at Wesleyan, the computer lab printed out hexagrams night after night while he was playing poker with colleagues at the Center for Advanced Studies.

For every event, Cage would refer to three charts consisting of sixty-four cells directly related to the sixty-four hexagrams of the *I Ching*. The charts referred to duration, dynamics, and sound. Sounds would only appear in the odd-numbered cells, silences in the even. This ensured that the piece would breathe and have a spacious quality. They included just about everything you can imagine: single notes, trills, unusual ways of playing—plucking, hitting the strings with sticks, chords of various density, and noises (hitting the piano lid). Dynamics appeared once every fourth cell, in sixteen increments from extremely soft (*pppp*) to extremely loud (*ffff*). If an empty cell came up, the previous dynamic continued. In addition Cage used the pedal not to color or blur certain passages but simply as a structural element. It occurs at unexpected times, even in the middle of a passage.

The score is laid out spatially: a quarter note equals 2½ centimeters from left to right on the page. In addition Cage randomly indicated accelerandos (speeding up) and decelerandos (slowing down) from point to point, overriding the spatial notation. Tudor consulted a mathematician to try to discover an accurate way of accomplishing this.

Cage consciously chose the sound materials; when a rhythmic cell came up, that rhythm would replace the rhythm of the chosen material. That is, the shapes of the written gestures are changed by the shapes of the durations. He also devised a lovely way of changing the shapes of melodic patterns, by replacing those shapes with those of different rhythmic patterns. So a melodic pattern would change shape in a sort of extreme theme and variations technique.

The layering of the many parameters and replacement procedures, as well as the variations in tempo, spatial notation, structural pedaling, and so on, give a deep seriousness to this music, dispelling the notion of sloppiness or carelessness that so many people attribute to chance music. It really isn't random at all in a certain sense. So much is chosen and controlled by the composer. So much is personal. No other music sounds like this; it sounds like Cage.

Music of Changes would have been impossible without the collaboration of pianist David Tudor. David had been trained as an organist as well as a pianist, and had an organist's mind-set and skill at predetermining chains of presets, which could be called upon with a flick of a wrist. Once I was assisting him in the recording of *Improvization Ajoutée*, a mammoth organ work by Mauricio Kagel that involved moving quickly from one set of mixtures to another. Another assistant who was knowledgeable about organ presets would suggest to Tudor easier ways of executing certain moves. Tudor would calmly demonstrate how his own choice made possible a set of moves two or three steps down the chain. I was amazed at his logical control of this complex instrument. He was like a master chess player who can see several steps ahead given all the possible moves of his opponent.

The story goes that Cage would compose a section of *Changes*, Tudor would work it out and, based on his decisions about playing, Cage would continue working. Later Cage would remark that Tudor was *The Music of Changes*.

Atlas Eclipticalis

John Cage composed most of *Atlas Eclipticalis* in 1961 while he was at Wesleyan as a Fellow at the Center for Advanced Studies. It's a work for orchestra with over eighty separate instrumental parts. Cage composed each part by overlaying transparent templates on the *Atlas Eclipticalis* star map, using the stars to give him note heads. In the 1950s, astronomers and physicists believed that the universe was random. So Cage used the stars as a source of randomness. He simply superimposed transparent sheets of paper over the star map and copied the dots.

There's no full score of the work. In a Beethoven symphony the score has all the instrumental parts written one above the other. *Atlas* doesn't have a full score because the instrumental parts are not synchronized; the players don't play at the same time. There are four pages that show the layout of the work. But Cage says they may not be useful, "since an *I-Ching* operation producing inactivity was subsequently made." The conductor chooses which parts are to be played, then marks those constellations that are in his ensemble. He studies the parts (any good conductor should do this) to give him an idea of the amount of activity and inactivity (silence) there is. He stands up in front of the orchestra and uses his arms like the hands of a clock. I think Cage is being a bit mischievous here. You say of a bad conductor that he is merely a timebeater. So Cage is asking the conductor to indicate time, nothing else, no expression. Furthermore, the conductor moves his arms at least twice as slow as clock time. It takes him two minutes or longer to get around the clock face. At 00″ he starts with his right hand raised above his head; at 15″ his arm is at 3 o'clock; at 30″ both arms join together straight down; then both arms move in opposite directions, the right moving counterclockwise back to 3 o'clock, the left to 9 o'clock, at 45″. Both join together above the head at 60″. It's wonderful the way time goes backward as well as at least twice as slow.

This brings up the whole notion of time in music. The romantic notion is that there is such a thing as musical or psychological time, which is created by the content and proportions of the music. But Cage, who inhabits the real world as described by Zen, prefers to use real or clock time in his music. If he slows it down or speeds it up, he does so directly and not in some psychological way.

In *Atlas* the players watch the conductor simply to be apprised of the passage of time. Each part has arrows that correspond to 0, 15, 30, 45, and 60 seconds on the clock face. Each part has four pages. Each page has five systems. Horizontal space equals time.

Vertical space equals frequency (pitch). The players' parts consist of notated pitches connected by lines. There are certain rules about playing notes separately, not making intermittent sounds (stars don't occur in repetitive patterns), and making changes in sound quality. No page is like any other, though all look similar. In a symphony orchestra the sixteen first violins usually play the same thing. In *Atlas*, nobody does.

There's no poetic reference to the heavens as there are in Gustav Holst's *The Planets*, for example, in which each movement is named for one of the seven planets: *Mars the Bringer of War*, *Venus the Bringer of Peace*, *Mercury the Winged Messenger*, *Jupiter the Bringer of Jollity*, and so forth. Holst was interested in astrology and read horoscopes. In *Atlas* there are no poetic references like that. There are a few whimsical ones, though. Most of the string parts may sound an octave higher than written. (The stars are high above us.) The conductor moves at half speed or slower to show universal time or timelessness. The sizes of the note heads determine the loudness of the sound. Most are small (the stars are distant). All of the sounds are produced in a normal manner.

Cage uses the word "constellation" to describe aggregates of pitches, as well as instrumental groupings. Individual tones within an aggregate may be played in any succession; their spacing need not refer to time. There's always silence between tones unless they are superimposed or interpenetrate, that is, one sound made while another is sounding. A string player can pluck a string with her left hand while bowing with her right. There are twenty instrumental groupings, labeled A to T. Constellation G, for example, consists of Violins 2, 4, 9; Contrabass 3; French horn 3; Trumpet 3; Trombone 2; Percussion 6 and 8; and Harp 1. There are thirty-three events.

I just came across a quotation from C. S. Lewis's book, *The Discarded Image*, which Art Upgren of the Wesleyan Astronomy Department used as an epigraph in his book, *Night Has a Thousand*

Eyes: "It is always necessary to remember that constellation in medieval language seldom means, as with us, a permanent pattern of stars. It usually means a temporary state of their relative positions."

Each part is dedicated to some friend of Cage's. The conductor's part is dedicated to Victor Butterfield, who was the president of Wesleyan at the time Cage wrote the piece. There are also dedications to Wesleyan professors and their spouses, including N. O. Brown (Philosophy) and Beth, Ross Gortner (Physics) and Priscilla, David McAllester (Music) and Susan, Louis Mink (Philosophy) and Pat, Joe Peoples (Geology) and Ruth, Norman Rudich (Romance Languages) and Ruth, Marian Vaine (Music Department secretary), Carl Viggiani (Romance Languages) and Jane, Richard K. Winslow (Music) and Betty. The rest are mostly composers, dancers, and artists, a *Who's Who* of the art world at that time. The dedications are a little sexist, I must admit. The wives' names are secondary. But this was the early Sixties and that was the mindset then. He probably wouldn't have done that later. In any event, the dedications taken as a whole form a constellation of Cage's friends at that time.

Leonard Bernstein conducted *Atlas* with the New York Philharmonic in 1968, along with works by Earle Brown and Morton Feldman. Bernstein was a conductor with an oversized ego. Feldman used to say he had a "poisenality problem." (Morty spoke with a heavy Brooklyn accent.) Bernstein gave a little speech before performing the three works, denigrating the music. It was embarrassing. Cage had decided to put contact microphones on many of the instruments. It's an option in the score. He might have thought of them as tiny telescopes that amplified the distant (soft) stars (sounds). You could buy them at Radio Shack for a couple of dollars in those days. They had no bass response and could break easily. Imagine asking professional players to attach cheap mikes to their expensive instruments. They hated it. Some of the players ripped them off and stamped on them. James Tenney acted as assistant to the conductor for this performance. His duty was to operate the volume and tone controls of the amplifiers from a part he made from another work, *Cartridge Music*. During the performance there was the biggest walkout in the Philharmonic's history. It was as if somebody had exploded a tear gas bomb inside the hall. Most of the audience came back after the intermission, though, to hear a Tchaikovsky symphony. At one point in the concert, Bernstein improvised with the orchestra. He went through all the clichés you've ever heard in symphonic music—crescendos, climaxes, abrupt startings and stoppings, dramatic pauses. He wanted to prove, you see, that he could accomplish the same results by improvisation. (Dumb.)

4

GRAPHIC NOTATION

The King of Denmark

Does anybody know why a piece of music would be called *The King of Denmark*? You would have to know something about the history of World War II. When the Nazis invaded Denmark they made all the Jewish people wear a yellow star on their sleeves. In protest, the King of Denmark wore a yellow star every time he went out in public. He was protesting the Nazi treatment of the Jews. So, in 1964, Morton Feldman, an American Jew, wrote a work called *The King of Denmark*. It's for one musician playing a battery of percussion instruments. In the early Sixties composers discovered that noisy, non-pitched instruments, such as cymbals, gongs, pieces of wood, anything that makes noise, could constitute a fruitful and exciting sound palette to explore. There were a whole slew of solo percussion pieces. Usually they were written for everything but the kitchen sink. (Sometime the kitchen sink, too.) The more sounds the better. (Recently composer-percussionist Stuart Saunders Smith advocated writing works for only one percussion instrument and programming concerts for ensembles of two or three instruments, much the same as chamber music concerts. He coined the phrase, "percussion ecology.") German composer Karlheinz Stockhausen's *Zyklus* (*Cycles*) is a germinal work in this genre. The performer is surrounded by a large battery of instruments, represented by a circular score. The player may start anywhere on the circle and move around from right to left or left to right, from instrument to instrument. It's a wonderful piece.

Most of these solo percussion pieces were loud and sounded a bit like electronic music. But in *The King of Denmark* Morton Feldman, lo and behold, asked the player to play with his fingertips, hands, and any part of the arm. You can't make a lot of noise by hitting a cymbal with your fingertips. Virtually every piece that Feldman wrote in thirty-five years was to be played *pianissimo*. His sound world was a quiet one. Why? Feldman had very poor eyesight; he was practically blind. He wore extremely thick eyeglasses and in order to see something up close, he had to remove his eyeglasses and squint. He had to use one hand to squeeze his eye into a certain position. When we would go out to Chinese restaurants with him in New York, he would always take us to brightly lit places. I think that Feldman's poor eyesight had something to do with his penchant for quiet sounds. I can't be sure. He had to look closely at things. He had to listen closely to sounds.

Let me tell a story about Tong Kin-woon, a *ch'in* player who was at Wesleyan several years ago. The *ch'in* is an ancient Chinese zither with silk strings. It makes lovely, quiet sounds. During the Ming Dynasty, it was played by scholars, gentlemen, and philosophers. Mr. Tong told me that they would not necessarily play for someone else. They would simply sit and play, meditating, not entertaining anybody. He explained that they might stop playing, too, and imagine the music going on. What a beautiful idea! The actual sounds exist in your mind. It puts a different focus on the music. Since the strings are made of silk, the sound is almost inaudible.

Once Tong presented a lecture-demonstration in the World Music Hall, a small space specially made for acoustic music. He was playing beautifully, but had amplified the instrument through a cheap sound system. The sound of silk strings through tinny loudspeakers sounded awful. Between pieces I asked him if he wouldn't mind playing the next piece unamplified; I wanted to hear the *ch'in*, if only once in my life, in its pristine state. I wanted

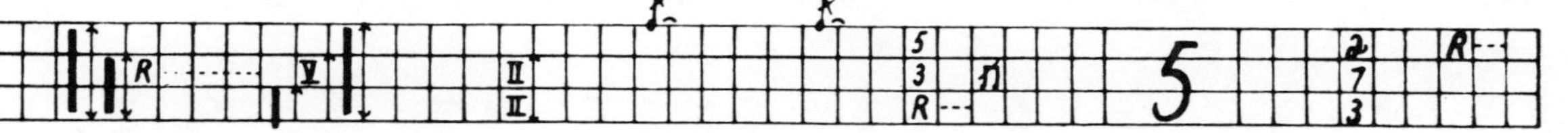

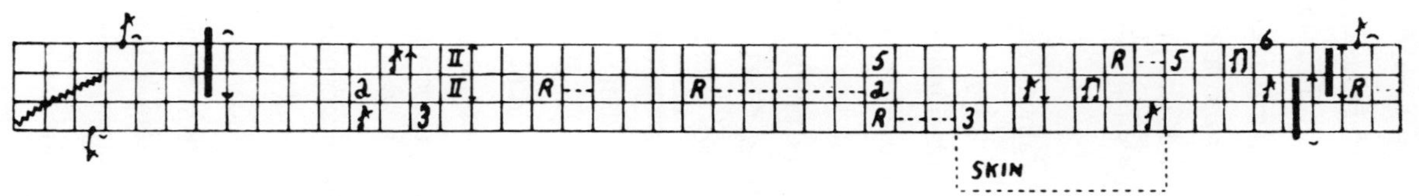

Example of the score of Morton Feldman's King of Denmark.
Copyright 1964 by C. F. Peters Corporation. Used by permission.

to hear it the way it sounded during the Ming Dynasty. He replied that we wouldn't be able to hear it. I asked him what would be so wrong with not hearing one piece of music among thousands one listens to in a lifetime. We constantly hear music we don't want to hear, in elevators, bookstores, supermarkets, on airplanes before takeoffs. I begged him to do it for me, and I was chair of the department at that time. So he did. It was just gorgeous! You heard the sound of silk. The audience sat there and leaned in toward the music.

The King of Denmark is graphically notated. There are three horizontal layers of boxes, designated high, middle, and low. Numbers in boxes indicate numbers of sounds in the boxes. Dynamics are soft and as equal as possible. This instantly eliminates any hint of dynamic contrast. The instruments are not specified precisely because it's unlikely that one percussionist will have exactly the same instruments as another. That's always been a problem with percussion. So Feldman gives general categories: *C* stands for cymbal; *G* for gong; *T* for timpano (kettledrum); *B*, bell-like sound; *S*, skin; and so forth. He told me once that he got the idea for this piece while sitting on the beach at Far Rockaway, Long Island. Occasionally the wind would blow sounds his way, fragments of conversations, music from transistor radios. You've had that experience haven't you? It's just beautiful when a little sound comes to you on the wind.

During the Fifties Feldman talked more to painters than he talked to musicians. His best friend was Philip Guston. There were long conversations at the Cedar Bar in New York among the great abstract painters—Pollack, Kline, de Kooning, Rothko. Feldman got a lot of ideas from them. The surface of the painting was where the painting was; the manner of applying paint to canvas was crucial. There were no hidden meanings.

5
TOWN HALL

The Swallows of Salangan

Morton Feldman's *The Swallows of Salangan* (1960) is a work for chorus and orchestra. The title was taken from *Safe Conduct*, a biographical essay by Boris Pasternak. Here is a passage that appears in Feldman's published score:

> I loved the living essence of historical symbolism, or, putting it another way, that instinct with the help of which we like Salangan swallows, built the world—an enormous nest, put together from the earth and sky, life and death, and two times, the ready to hand and the defaulting. I understood that it was prevented from crumbling by the strength of its links, consisting in the transparent figurativeness of all its parts.

I conducted the first American performance of *Swallows* in 1963 in Town Hall, New York. The Brandeis Chamber Chorus, of which I was director, had been invited to participate in a concert of the works of Morton Feldman and Earle Brown. It was sponsored by The Foundation for Contemporary Performance Arts. John Cage and Merce Cunningham were on the board of directors. There were wonderful musicians in the orchestra: Max Neuhaus and Paul Price played vibraphones, John Cage and David Tudor were the pianists. (Some orchestra.)

All instruments and voices begin together; then each person proceeds at his or her own speed. All I had to do was give the downbeat, then stand there while the slowly changing sonic landscape unfolded. Since there was no tempo or meter, there was no definite speed at which the upbeat should be given. In conventional music, the tempo of the upbeat should be the same as that of the movement to be played. A good conductor will show the players the tempo by giving them an upbeat in that tempo. Therefore, I felt no compulsion to be absolutely precise but simply to indicate to the players when the work would begin.

What happens when you let each performer choose the durations of the sounds? They gradually spread apart, going out of phase with each other. The further they go, the harder it is to hear what came before. Time erases memory. You know how it is when you look at clouds. As they move across the sky, they change shape. Or when you're driving across the country, as you come up over a hill, for example, mountains seem to change their relationships with each other. They seem to move as your perspective changes. Artists know about this phenomenon. An object changes shape as the angle of light that illuminates it changes.

The orchestra consists of six woodwinds, eight brass, eleven strings, two pianos, harp, guitar, and two vibraphones, as well as a chorus of eighteen singers. There are thirty-six separate parts. Most of the chords are made up of tone clusters, the individual notes of which are spread out and distributed throughout the orchestra and chorus. The opening chord consists of a cluster of five semitones: A, B-flat, B-natural, C, and D-flat. But it is spaced out over a range of four octaves. The chorus by itself encompasses more than two octaves. Between the bass, tenor, alto, and soprano are symmetrical intervals of a minor ninth; the tenor and alto parts are compressed into a three-note cluster, which covers only a minor third. Such a lovely symmetry. By starting with a neutral five-tone cluster, Feldman expresses the color of each instrument, as well as the simultaneities, free of functionality.

Feldman loved the music of the Austrian composer, Anton Webern. Webern had been a student of Arnold Schoenberg, who developed the notorious and misunderstood twelve-tone system of

Page 1 of The Swallows of Salangan *by Morton Feldman.*

composition. In this system, all twelve notes of the scale are equal, and because of this, music of a highly dissonant texture results. In order to avoid tonality, consonant intervals—thirds in particular—are used sparingly. Dissonant intervals—seconds, sevenths, ninths—are emphasized. By avoiding tonality, one more easily perceives tone color, density, and spaciousness. Webern's music is characterized by wide intervals and single tones surrounded by silences. By separating tones in this way, attention is focused on the sounds themselves, not on their relationships. There are no climaxes in *Swallows*, just regions along the way where everybody comes together. I am reminded of oases scattered across a desert landscape. On page two, the sopranos have seven high A's, doubled by three flutes, trumpets, tuba, vibraphones, and pianos. Such a beautiful color!

I remember the ending of that Town Hall performance: Max Neuhaus had a vibraphone solo. The vibraphone has a long decay time and he must have been moving slower than the other vibraphone player, too. Feldman didn't plan it that way, but it was beautiful. In classical pieces there is often a coda (Italian for tail), which serves to dissipate the energy that has been built up. In Feldman's *Durations III*, a set of pieces for small chamber ensembles, a solo tuba meanders about at the end of one of the pieces. Feldman writes that in. In *Swallows* it happens by chance. No matter how they were put into motion, the results are uncannily beautiful.

Christian Wolff in Cambridge

The title of the next work will probably confuse you. It's called *Christian Wolff in Cambridge* (1963). I like to play it because it refers to Christian Wolff, one of the main composers we're going to study, and because I happen to know a story about how Morty got the idea for it. In the early Sixties Christian Wolff was a classics tutor at Harvard. Feldman was impressed. (He had never gone to college.) Once he visited Christian in his office in Claverly Hall. The door was partially open and Christian was sitting inside reading Euripides. That's a beautiful image, don't you think? Several years later, when I was teaching at Brandeis and had been visiting Feldman in New York, he asked me for a ride to Cambridge, to visit Christian. On the way out of New York, in my Volkswagen Bug, Feldman remarked: "Lucier, you drive like Beethoven." I asked him what he meant. He replied: "You're always changing lanes!" When we arrived at Claverly Hall, Christian's door was partly open and there he was, sitting in the same chair reading Euripides. Two identical situations, several years apart. It had a sort of timelessness not unlike studying classical Greek literature.

The Brandeis Chamber Chorus got an offer to make a recording of contemporary choral music for CBS. I wrote to Morty and asked him for a piece. He asked me what the range of my chorus was. I told him that we had a couple of sopranos who could get up to a high B-flat and a few of our basses could go as low as E-flat or thereabouts. He replied that he didn't want to know what the highest and lowest notes were, but what were the comfortable ranges. He didn't want to know the extremes.

In the early Sixties composers were exploring—I almost said "exploiting"—the possibilities of the human voice and musical instruments. In 1965 Karlheinz Stockhausen wrote *Momente*, a large-scale work for chorus and instruments in which the singers clap their hands and bodies, yell, scream, laugh, play little percussion instruments, giggle, murmur, shout, and so forth. In *Number 5 Zeitmasse*, five wind players play as fast as possible. Much of the music of this ilk was grotesque and overheated. Morty's music was in a temperate zone. He wasn't at the North Pole or the South Pole. I gave him the range of the average college chorus. He sent me *Christian Wolff in Cambridge*.

It's a short, simple *a cappella* choral work, in two sections: *A* and *A′*. Each consisted of exactly the same twenty chords and single tones. The only difference between the sections is that the second part has crescendo-decrescendo (inhale-exhale) markings under the second and sixth chords, plus *fermatas* over the first and second-to-last chord, as well as a single bass D-flat. *Fermatas*, also known as birds' eyes, are symbols indicating sounds to be held for an indefinite length of time. In classical music they are often used for dramatic purposes: holding a dominant seventh chord before returning to the main theme, for example. But with Feldman they're simply a means to lengthen a sound. You don't anticipate the next sound; you listen a little longer to the one that's being held. Otherwise, the music in the two sections is identical. Perhaps the second time Morty visited Christian, there was a breeze coming through a window or his door was open a crack more.

In conducting Feldman the weights of the sounds are crucial. If, for example, the altos are in the high part of their range, they run out of air a little sooner than the rest of the singers. You don't wait until they do, but you listen for it. You can feel the sound crumble. You sense a hidden drama. At that moment you give the next downbeat. You don't cut the sound off cleanly, as you often do in choral music, you simply move from one chord to the next. Conducting Feldman consists of listening and waiting. Any musician knows that chords have different weights according to how they're spaced. In eighteenth-century harmony, if the root of a chord is in the bass, the chord is stable and heavy. If the third is in the bass, the chord is lighter. Everyone who studies harmony becomes sensitive to the weights of chords. I've often thought of Feldman's attacks as similar to the stratified rock one sees while driving on modern highways that have been cut through rock. You can see geological time in those strata. Every time I drive down Route 9 towards Old Saybrook I see the cuts in the rock they made to construct the highway and think of Feldman's attacks. If you listen carefully to his soft attacks you can hear individual instruments "speak." It takes each one an almost imperceptibly different time to sound. It's as if he's magnified the minute differences in timing.

There is one place in the recorded performance where we were a little bit off; we sang a near-octave where there should have been a minor ninth. But it didn't seem to bother Morty. Absolute perfection is not paramount in this music. The dichotomy between precision and imprecision goes back to Debussy. You write your music as precisely as you can, but the performance is human.

Afternoon of a Faun

When I think about Earle Brown's *From Here* (1963) I also think of Debussy's *Afternoon of a Faun* (1892–1894, published in 1895), I'm not sure exactly why. It really doesn't make a lot of sense, but somehow I think there's some logic there. I'm going to go with my instincts and not with any idea of what I've previously learned or known. It has to do with their respective forms.

It seems to me that composers can do one of two things in making a work: one is to use a pre-existing form and simply fill it in, the other is to expand or invent new forms by inventing a new system or by intuition. You can do that with a simple ABA song form, for example. The same music appears in the A sections, bisected by a contrasting B section. Dante's *terza rima* has that structure: the first and third lines have the same rhyme, the middle line, which is different, becomes the first and third line rhymes of the next tercet. ABA forms seem to be basic in much Western music. Most pop music songs are in ABA form. Over time the simple song form got expanded into sonata form. The first movements of the Mozart piano sonatas, for example, follow more or less this similar form: an exposition consisting of two themes, the first in the tonic key, that is, the key that defines the sonata movement as a whole; the second in the dominant key, that is, a fifth above the tonic. The first theme is often assertive and angular, the second smoother and more graceful. (We used to call them masculine and feminine but we don't anymore.) The exposition is repeated so the listener is convinced by what he has heard.

What follows is a development section in which the composer transforms the material in themes A and B in various ways—fragmentation, juxtaposition, adventurous changes in harmony, and so forth. This is where he shows his skill. After the development is over (tired out, you might say), the exposition is recapitulated, but this time the second theme is in the tonic key. You are home again. Some recent theorists have suggested that sonata form developed as an analog to colonialism: after traveling to a foreign land and developing (exploiting) raw material you find there, you come home where it is comfortable.

Recently there have been at least two kinds of fraud in recording classical sonata form works. One is by recording the exposition only once in order to save space on the recording; the other is to record it once but copy it so that it sounds as if it had been played twice. All of this is to save time in the recording session. The first assumes that there is no structural reason to repeat the exposition; the second assumes that the repeat can be exactly the same as the original, that no variation in tempo, phrasing, or articulation should be made. Both are egregious violent activities comparable to slashing the *Mona Lisa*.

Some composers design their own forms before the actual act of composition and simply fill them in. John Cage did that with early percussion pieces such as his *First Construction (In Metal)* (1939). The piece consists of sixteen units of sixteen measures each. Each unit is organized in groups of four, three, two, three, and four measures. The overall form of the work is composed of four, three, two, three, and four sixteen-measure units, too. So the work is built on a square root idea. Once Cage determined the form he simply filled in the musical material in a predetermined order. The overall form, however, is a bit more complicated than that. Cage included references to sonata form by describing the first four sixteen-measure sections as the exposition, followed by a development section. He even added a nine-measure coda at the end. The various sections consist of sixteen motives arranged in four circles of four motives each. Throughout the work Cage felt free to move in either direction around the circles, repeating some of them at his discretion. So the form of the work is a hybrid of four formal ideas: palindrome, square root, sonata, and circle.

For other composers — Morton Feldman, for example — form may be more intuitive. Morty used to say that he simply wrote one chord, forgot about it, wrote another, forgot about that one, and so forth. In many of his (mostly later) works, however, Feldman used repetitive structures, each repetition a little rhythmically or melodically different. He had a collection of Turkish rugs whose designs were in some ways similar. Done by weavers from memory; the repetitions often weren't exact. In any case, there seem to be prevailing thoughts about form in each historical era, even if a composer thinks that he or she is free of such constraints. Perhaps it's only natural to fall into patterns. They describe the era that one is in. Erik Satie wrote a *Piece in the Form of a Pear*.

One of the things Satie was responsible for was structuring music without a climax. In *Vexations* (1893) for piano a phrase is repeated 840 times without pause. It's usually performed with a bunch of pianists. It's hard to imagine a single player sitting at the piano and playing one phrase over eight hundred and forty times. Satie wrote a beautiful piece, *The Death of Socrates* (1918), for a singer and piano or orchestra, taken from the dialogues of Plato. Socrates who, you will remember, had been convicted of corrupting the youth of Athens, kills himself by drinking hemlock. Instead of making a romantic opera on the death of Socrates, Satie sets the words as if someone's simply telling it. Because it's sung, the music rises and falls, following the text, as in Gregorian chant, but there are no real climaxes, at his death or anyplace else. As Socrates is dying, he feels his legs get cold from the feet up. At a certain point the music simply stops. A cool way of depicting death. He got the idea from looking at pictures of ancient Greek buildings, including the Parthenon, which are now completely white. When they were built these buildings were brightly colored. We've blanched out that ancient culture; it's been whitened out so there isn't any color. We think of it as pure.

Debussy's *Prelude to the Afternoon of a Faun* is one of the germinal works of the twentieth century. (Actually, it was written in 1898.) A faun (not fawn) is a mythical being, half human, half animal. Debussy got the idea from a work by the symbolist poet Stephane Mallarmé, of the same title. The symbolist poets were interested in suggestion, evanescent ideas, fleeting thoughts, remembering something several times—each time a little different, sort of light, whimsical, wisps of fog, slathers of sunlight. The idea of rigid or coherent structure or works with development sections did not interest them. Structures were breaking down in favor of the psychological, memories. I think we all do that in a certain way; it is part of our thinking. I've been doing yoga recently and when I try to meditate, thoughts pop into my mind from out of nowhere. I don't know where they come from. Sometimes I think of somebody I haven't thought about for thirty years. I might be able to push a thought out of my mind for a while but it often comes back and when it does it's slightly different.

Afternoon of a Faun almost defies analysis. To be sure, you can hear things that occurred before, but they often come back in a different form. The opening flute melody returns several times, each time slightly altered, and always on a different chord. First the flute comes in unaccompanied on a mid-range C-sharp; then as a dissonant major seventh; later as the sixth degree of a chord on E; then as an added sixth on a dominant ninth chord on E. Every time the melody appears it is harmonized differently. It comes in a different form, too. It's like a fleeting memory.

The opening flute solo is supposed to sound like the Greek

panpipe. In the ballet, this half-human and half-animal creature wishes he were human. He comes upon a group of nymphs for whom he has erotic feelings, but for obvious reasons it can never be. The opening melody descends like a drooping fern, a musical example of geotropism, the tendency for plants to bend toward the earth. It's the basic visual design, you might say, in Art Deco. The points of repose throughout the piece, that is, places where one gets the feeling of closure, where forward motion partially stops, remind me of the Fibonacci (Italian mathematician, b. 1170) series, a number system that describes the way certain things in nature grow.

Each spiral of a seashell, for example, grows in the form of the Fibonacci series, in which you simply add the two previous numbers to get the next, for example, 1, 2, 3, 5, 8, 13, 21, and so forth. I look at the score of *Afternoon of a Faun* and I see that it doesn't exactly follow the series, but it has the same feeling of growth. The beginnings of the main sections occur at measures 30, 37, 55, 79, and 94. This nine-minute piece feels like a natural growing organism.

From Here

Usually when you analyze a musical work you have to take it apart to discover what it is made of. In Earle Brown's *From Here* you have to do the opposite; you put it together. The score is disassembled. Let's look at the instructions and the instrumentation. It is scored for voices and instruments. Actually, it was originally composed for instruments only, but when Earle learned that the Brandeis Chamber Chorus was going to participate in the Town Hall concert he added the choral parts. For those of you who don't know music, don't be intimidated. SATB means soprano, alto, tenor, and bass singing voices. The orchestra consists of flute, oboe, E-flat clarinet (a smaller version of the clarinet that you may know), B-flat clarinet (which is the normal one), bass clarinet, bassoon, French horn, B-flat trumpet, trombone, tuba, piano, harp, amplified guitar, and two percussionists. One percussionist plays a glockenspiel (that high little bell instrument that you often see in a marching band, only this is laid out flat), marimba (a large, wooden xylophone instrument), and timpani or kettledrums. The other plays xylophone, vibraphone, and timpani. Then we have a pair of violins, a viola, a cello, and a double bass. The piece lasts from ten to twenty minutes.

In the *Preliminary Notes* Earle talks about spontaneous decisions in the performance. He uses the word *mobile*. We all know what a mobile is, do we not? The mobile was the invention of sculptor Alexander Calder who hung thin metal plates of various shapes up in the air on wires. The shapes are fixed, but the relationships among them constantly change because of air currents. He made so many mobiles that when he made fixed sculptures he had to call them *stabiles*. There's a stabile in Hartford. One mayor of the city hated it. Every day he looked out his office window and saw the Calder stabile. He wanted the city to haul it away. Fortunately he was beaten in the next election. The mayor left, the Calder stayed. That's politics.

Another inspiration for Earle Brown was Jackson Pollock, the inventor of action painting. He was famous for those beautiful drip paintings. He would lay canvases flat on the floor and drip paint on them. They were brilliant, exciting, violent. The spontaneous application of paint on the canvas gives you a result that you would not get otherwise. More important is that every part of the painting looked the same. They are sometimes referred to as "all-over" paintings.

Earle Brown had been a jazz musician as well as a recording engineer. He liked the spontaneous give and take among jazz musicians, as distinct from symphony players who simply show up and do what they're told. In *From Here* the conductor(s) is (are) responsible for the structure of the work.

The score consists of four pages, three for the instrumentalists, one for the chorus. There are fourteen events for the instrumentalists. Ten are notated more or less conventionally; four are graphic. On each page there are large numbers 1, 2, 3, 4, 5 and 1, 2, 3, 4. Let's look at page one. Events 1, 2, 3, 4, and 5 are fairly precisely fixed. Let's look at the first flute-oboe part in the upper left-hand corner. There's an F-sharp, and then a thick line and a fermata. A fermata, as we know, indicates that a sound is to be held an indefinite length of time. You can hear that the flute sustains the F-sharp as long as the conductor indicates. If she runs out of breath, she simply plays it again. All the parts are cued by the conductor. The page numbers are printed large on pieces of cardboard, which, loosely bound, hang over the conductor's stand so that the players can see them. The conductor simply flips them over to the appropriate page. Then, if he wants to start with Event 1, for example, he raises one finger. If he wants Events 1 and 2 to be played in sequential order, he raises the first, then the second finger. If he wants to mix 1 and 2, he indicates 1 with one hand, 2 with the other. The conductor may also cue players individually simply by pointing. He also indicates cut-offs. When he wants you to begin again, he makes a circular gesture. The conductor may also modify an event. Say a player is sustaining a sound. The conductor could give her a crescendo signal, making the sound grow in volume, followed by a diminuendo and a cut-off. These are some of the signals that the conductor uses to assemble the piece.

Let's look at Event 5 on page 2, scored for clarinets, bass clarinet, bassoon, horn, trumpet, trombone, and tuba. The four instruments on top are making sounds with the keys of their instruments. I remember that the French horn player during one of the rehearsals expressed disapproval of having to do this. Earle simply explained that if the sounds were in the percussion section, it wouldn't bother him.

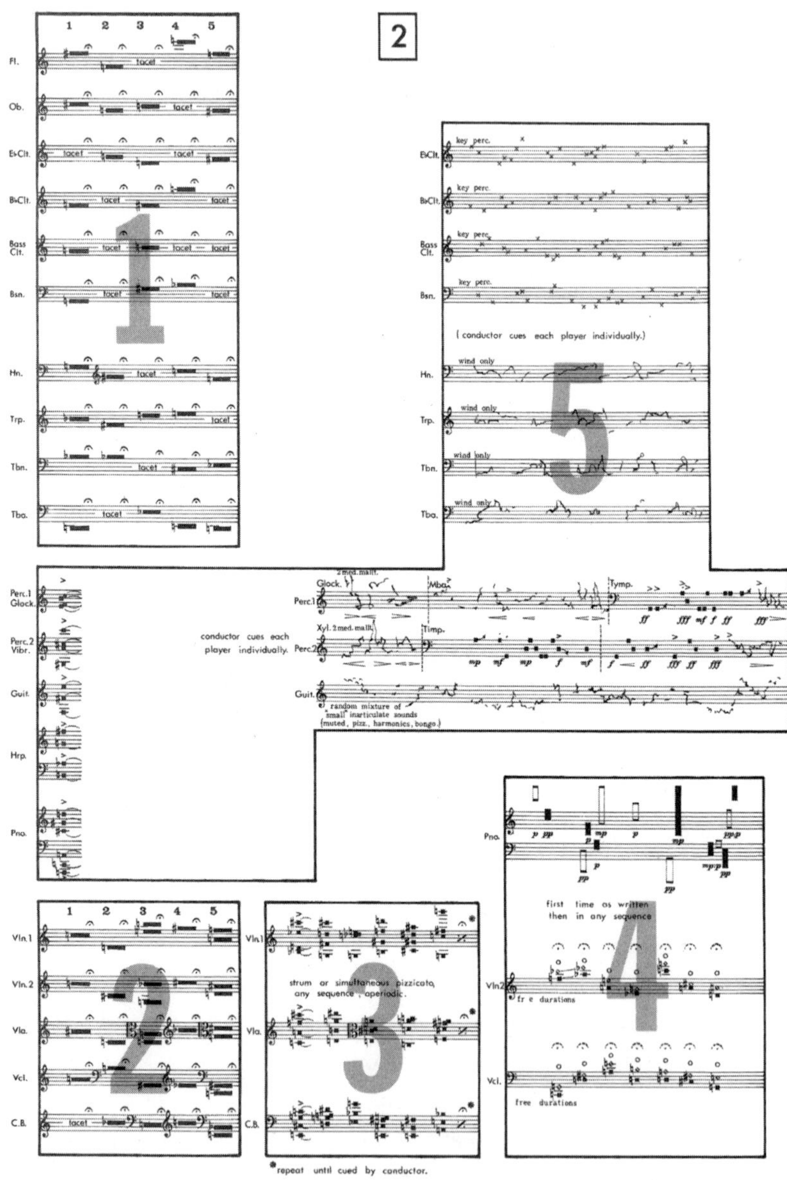

Page 2 from From Here *by Earl Brown. Copyright © by C. F. Peters / Henry Litoff's Music Publishers Frankfurt/M. Reprint by permission.*

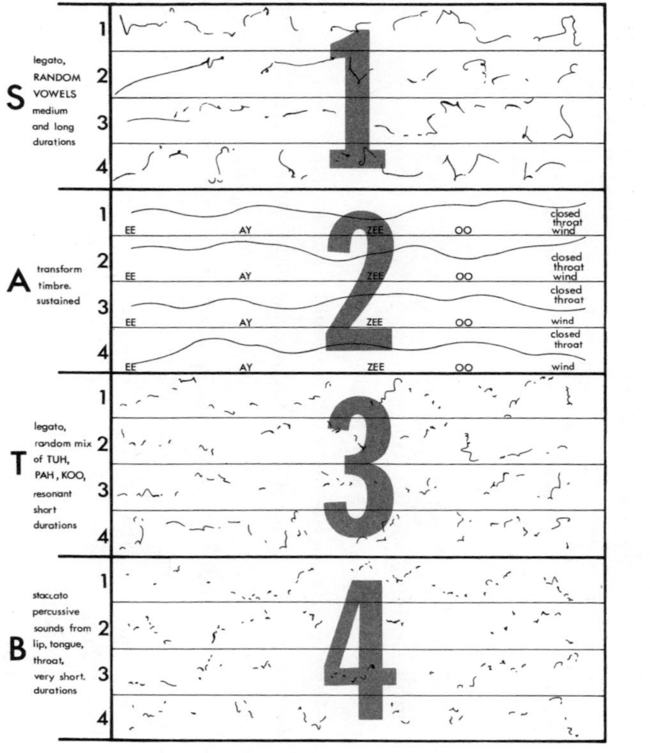

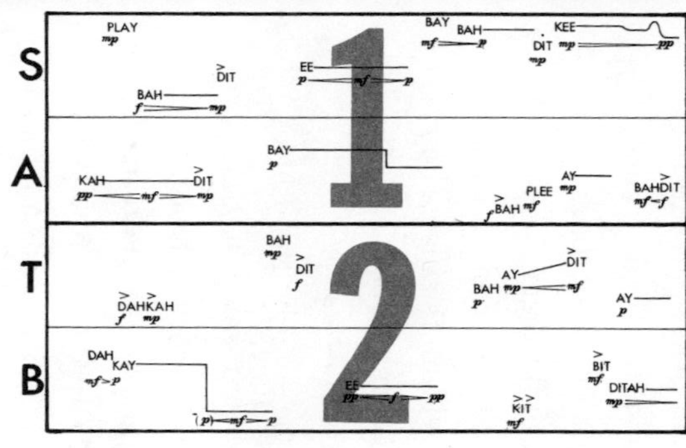

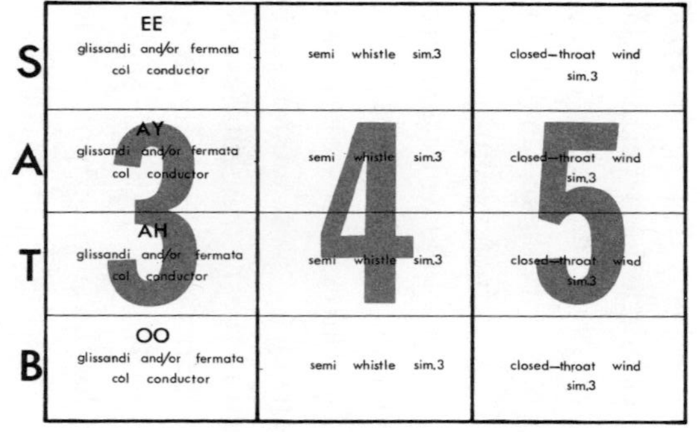

Choral parts of From Here. *Copyright 1972 by C. F. Peters Corporation. Used by permission.*

Those black rectangular symbols in the piano part are tone clusters. Earle doesn't explain them in the instructions. A cluster is a type of chord made up of any number of adjacent tones. That high one, since the rectangle is open, is diatonic, that is, it's played on the white notes on the piano. The filled-in one is chromatic, it consists of all the white and black notes within its range. Henry Cowell was the inventor of the tone cluster. In his book, *New Musical Resources*, he describes several types of clusters.

The choral parts are not supposed to be sung by themselves, whereas the instrumental parts may be performed separately. The chorus is traditionally divided into soprano, alto, tenor, and bass parts. By notating the choral parts graphically, he made it easy for the singers. You can't ask a singer to hit an F-sharp out of the blue unless he or she has perfect pitch. She needs another pitch to refer to. The sopranos sing legato (smooth), random vowels. The altos sing "ee, ay, oo" in a "closed-throat wind." You close your throat and produce a wind sound. The basses sing staccato percussive sounds from the lip, tongue, throat, very short. Over here they have specific sounds to sing, "bah," "dit," "ee." It's written in spatial notation. The one on the lower right has slides and/or fermata with the conductor. I had lots of fun with that one. (I was the choral conductor in the performance.) If everyone in the chorus is sliding you can cut them off, and make them go in and out, and so forth. This symbol indicates a semi-whistle. Earle would cue me, that is, tell me when I should come in. He would point to me and I would start conducting. He didn't know what I was going to conduct, though. That was my choice. Sometimes I would pretend I didn't see him when he wanted to cut me off so I could continue doing what I was enjoying.

In *From Here*, Earle Brown gives a great deal of authority to the conductor. Perhaps that's why his music gets played so much in Europe. European conductors enjoy performing it. It's a wonderful piece to program; you shouldn't over-rehearse it if you want to keep its freshness. Each player must know what the symbols mean, and possess a good technique to achieve those sounds. Good musicians can elicit sounds from their instruments that students can't. I had some wonderful singers, particularly sopranos, in my student chorus that year. After the performance, one of the parents came up to me and said, "Professor Lucier, music is my life, and this is not music!" She was horrified. That was long ago, in 1963.

From Here is one of the first open form works. It's got that quality of fragmentation. It seems to have a narrative but it's interrupted. There are beautiful flashes of sound. Once you've heard *From Here* a couple of times, you can recognize the various sections and hear the superimpositions. The conductor may operate in two ways: he may more or less plan out the length and structure of a performance; or, he may not plan at all but make unexpected decisions, quickly moving to unexpected places. This gives the performance an improvisatory quality one does not achieve in totally indeterminate music. Everything may be up to chance in a Cage work; Christian Wolff's early pieces rely on coordinations. In *From Here* the composer gives the musicians more or less precise materials, but the form is determined by the conductor.

6

ROSE ART MUSEUM

0′ 00″

In 1965 Sam Hunter, Director of the Rose Art Museum at Brandeis, invited John Cage to come up for a concert. I called Cage. He agreed and suggested we include a work of Christian Wolff, who was teaching at nearby Harvard, as well as a work of mine. I told him I would be happy to include a work of Christian's but was unsure about including something of my own. I hadn't been composing much at that time and told him so. I could hear mild disbelief on the other end of the telephone line. I then said that I had been working with a brain wave amplifier in an effort to make a work using brain waves but that I couldn't get the amp to work consistently. Cage laughed and said that it didn't matter whether it worked or not but that the intention to try it was what was important. With Cage's encouragement and a deadline to meet, I started thinking seriously about making a work for brain waves and resolved to get to work.

The concert began before the audience came in with Cage performing *0′ 00″* (1962). He was seated on the small landing between the two floors of the museum in a squeaky old armchair he had brought with him from Stony Point. We had affixed contact mikes to the chair, as well as to a typewriter he used to write letters. The idea of the piece is that you engage in an activity you have to do anyway and amplify it. Cage at that time was fixed on the notion that music was work. He saw around him flagrant examples of wishy-washy pieces by lazy composers. He also had a microphone around his throat, the kind used by World War II

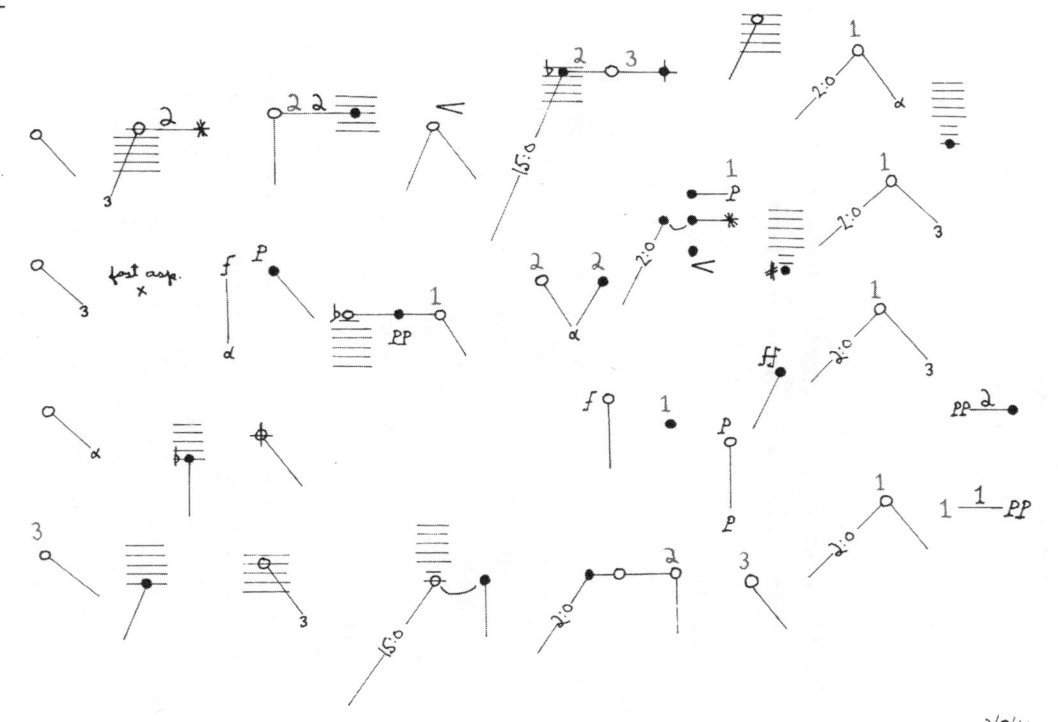

Page 4 of For 1, 2, or 3 people *by Christian Wolff.*
Copyright 1964 by C. F. Peters Corporation. Used by permission.

pilots. From time to time he would drink from a glass of water. The sounds of swallowing would be greatly amplified and emanate from loudspeakers positioned around the museum. So the sound material for the work consisted of amplified chair, typewriter and human swallowing. *0′ 00″* is a companion piece to *4′ 33″*. Both are prose scores.

For 1, 2, or 3 people

After the audience had come in John, Christian Wolff, and I performed *For 1, 2, or 3 people* (1964) by Christian Wolff. John played a musical saw, Christian an electric guitar, and I an amplified cymbal. The first thing you notice about *For 1, 2, or 3 people* is the title. Why did he use the word " people" and not "players" or "performers"? It's because the piece is meant for anybody to play, amateurs as well as professionals. The score consists of ten pages. You may play any number of them, repeating none, or any one repeated no more than ten times. This instruction reminds me a little of *Cartridge Music*, for which there are shapes on the pages for the same number of players. This is different, though; it controls the kind of material to be played, depending on how many pages are to be played. By playing the same page ten times, you hear the same materials in different combinations and continuity; you get into the material by surveying it in different contexts. Playing several pages once each you hear different but similar material in the same way. In a sense, the first activity could be thought of as vertical, the second, horizontal. The players are instructed to play all that is notated on a page. You don't repeat anything. You may start wherever you want. You don't read the notes from left to right, as you would in a Mozart sonata. It's not linear.

First, you have to learn Christian's vocabulary. Black notes are variously short, up to about a second; white notes are any length. This may be confusing because in conventional notation black notes are usually short, white notes, long. When you see a white note you must remember that it's not necessarily long and may be determined by the requirements of coordination. Notes with stems as sixteenth notes are very short. A diagonal line toward a note indicates a sound played directly after a preceding sound. You coordinate with the sound that came before. A diagonal line going away from a sound indicates that that note must be followed directly by another. If you play a sound and have a diagonal line how do you know when or if it's going to be followed by another? You have to think about that and solve it somehow. A vertical line down from a note means to play simultaneously with the next sound you hear, both the attack and release. It's a wonderful instruction because it's virtually impossible. By the time the sound occurs, you're already late. The slightly staggered effect doesn't sound ragged, as if it's a simultaneity played sloppily. It has a different sound quality. You can hear it.

Igor Stravinsky was fond of writing difficult parts for string players, including awkward double stops. *Double stop* is the term for two, three, or four notes played at the same time on adjacent strings. It's fairly easy to bow two or even three notes simultaneously, but since the strings are curved across the bridge of the instrument, you have to bow up or down in an arpeggio. Once during a rehearsal with the Boston Symphony, Richard Burgin, the concertmaster at that time, suggested to Stravinsky that they divide the pitches in a particularly difficult double stop, giving one note to half the violin section, the other to the other half. He explained that it would be easier and would sound the same. Stravinsky replied that he wanted the athleticism of playing it as is and that it would sound different. The means of production make it sound slightly different. That's what he wanted.

Here is a quote from Christian's set of instructions:

> A small number at the end of a line (e.g., at left top of I) = coordinate with the second (if the number is 2; third if 3, etc.) sound,

preceding (if diagonal line towards note), following after one has begun one's note (if diagonal line away from it), or play simultaneously with the second next sound (if the line is vertical).

If a line to a note is broken by a number followed, after a colon, by a zero, (—2:0—) (e.g., top middle of III), that number of seconds of silence intervene before the required coordination.

Let's look at a few of the other symbols. A delta sign (fourth letter of the Greek alphabet) at the end of a line indicates that the coordination must be made with a sound made by another player. If only one person is playing, they have to do it either with a sound they hear in the environment or a sound they've made unintentionally. Christian is providing for performances by one person. An *x* indicates you can play anything. A small black circle with an upward arrow tells you to make a sound that's high in some aspect. Not necessarily high in pitch, it could be a low pitch if somehow the overtones were high. You could do that electronically. He doesn't say high in relation to something else. He says high in some aspect. You could stand up on a ladder and play. You could simply play a high note. What else is high in some aspect? It could be a tone played sharp. To say high in some aspect is more interesting than simply saying play a high sound. It makes you think about sound, doesn't it?

A triangle indicates a sound in some respect dissonant with what immediately precedes it. So the whole question of dissonance arises. Throughout music history the classification of dissonance has evolved. What sounded harsh in one era is not so harsh in another. How can you tell if the note you play will be dissonant? In some respect it's got to be dissonant with the sound that immediately precedes it. So if another player is playing a C-natural, you might play a C-sharp. How do you know they are playing a C-natural?

Some people have perfect pitch. They often become piano tuners. They can tell what note is on a piano before they can see it. And if you don't have perfect pitch you could make your sound dissonant in some other way. If it's a pure tone, you could make a scratchy one. You have to think about it. That's why it's a wonderful and interesting piece. You can't take for granted the basic terminology of music, for example, what is high, what is dissonant.

A diamond indicates a harmonic, a technical term denoting an overtone or partial. On a stringed instrument you can lightly touch a string at a certain point and a silvery, pure sound comes out. *Asp* means play as fast as possible; *wd* stands for a sound using wood; *met*, metal; *t*, a sound made by tapping, touching, or tracing; *b*, a sound made by breathing or blowing, but not singing; *fr*, a sound involving friction; *sn*, snapping. One page of instructions explains the coordinations of the sounds, the other how to make them.

When I play this work I mark up my score to remind myself what the coordinations are as well as what sounds to make. I don't want to make mistakes. I don't want to appear incompetent. As you wait for something to happen, you're attentive in a way that you're not in any other circumstance. It's not like jazz where you have to think fast, or orchestral playing where you follow a conductor. It's a different social situation: you're playing and listening for another sound which may be a cue for you to make a sound, which in turn may be a cue for a third player.

To make a master score beforehand of what you're going to do is completely contrary to the intention of the piece. Anyway, it wouldn't do you much good if a cue leads you to something you couldn't have planned. Say my cue is a vertical line down from an open note head. It means play simultaneously with the next sound that I hear. I wait for the next sound. When it comes, I play it as simultaneously with that sound as I can. It's virtually impossible to achieve that degree of quickness but I follow my cues to the best of my ability.

It could happen that when you're supposed to play simultaneously or wait for the next couple of sounds, you could use sounds from the environment, even if there are three people, because you could have a situation where everyone is waiting for the next sound. If you get to an impasse the piece could be over. I suppose if you came to an impasse after performing only thirty seconds you could wait until enough time passes, then start again. You certainly have to do that if you're performing alone. There are no hard and fast rules, but you should follow the spirit of the work. There's a beautiful solo performance of *For 1, 2, or 3 people* by David Tudor. He recorded it on a small Baroque organ owned by the sculptor Richard Lippold. If my memory serves me correctly he recorded one version and then overdubbed a second one against it. It's not a typical performance of *For 1, 2, or 3 people* but it's absolutely lovely.

Christian has often said that his notation is the only way to get what he wants. It's not randomness or indeterminacy causing performance practice problems, it's the feeling of two or three players coordinating and being socially—no, that's the wrong word—being attentive and responsive to each other. It's very different from being in an orchestra where a conductor gives a downbeat and you're expected to come in on time. Those are two different phenomena.

For 1, 2, or 3 people is perfect chamber music, the essence of which is that you listen carefully to other players. Chamber music is played by small groups of people. The players rehearse a lot; they're not tied to a strict schedule of the orchestra. I've watched chamber musicians discuss for hours fine points of intonation and articulation, arguing about the intonation of a single chord. It has often been an amateur activity, too. If you had lived in the nineteenth century you probably would have played chamber music. I've always thought that Christian's coordinations evoke the best qualities of chamber music. There's no one in this room who couldn't perform this piece beautifully if she were serious about it.

When John Cage, Christian Wolff, and I performed *For 1, 2, or 3 people* at Wesleyan in 1988 John suggested we use balloons. You can make wonderful sounds with balloons by rubbing them. We all played around a grand piano. Christian decided that we'd play four pages, I, IV, V, and IX (Roman numerals). Christian marked off sections of each page for each of us. John usually got the left side, Christian, the right; I got the middle.

The University used to publish a calendar every year with photographs of professors for each month, sort of like the *Playboy* calendar. I've been teaching for twenty-five years and my picture never appeared in any of these publications. They're usually filled with pictures of science professors scribbling theorems on blackboards. Guess what picture got into the next year's graduate catalog? Professor Alvin Lucier blowing up a balloon! I finally made it. That's fine with me.

Music for Solo Performer

At that time (1965) I was not composing music. I had recently returned from Europe where I had heard a great deal of contemporary music. Even though I admired most of it I realized that it wasn't for me. It was too European. If I imitated it I would only be talking in a dialect. My mind was a blank, which was good because then I could let ideas come into it unobstructed by previous notions of what music should be. Around this time I met Edmond Dewan, a scientist who was working for the Air Force over at nearby Hanscom Air Base. Dewan was a passionate amateur organist. He had a huge organ in his home. He had been trying to interest Brandeis faculty composers in using his brain wave apparatus for musical purposes. No one was interested; perhaps they thought it was a gimmick. At that time Brandeis owned a synthesizer—an Arp 2600—but it didn't interest me much. I just didn't like the sounds it produced. The waveforms were too periodic and any means to override this condition weren't successful enough for me. So I took Dewan up on his offer. I borrowed his Tektronix differential amplifier and got to work in the Electronic Music Studio housed in the basement of the Brandeis Library. I would go in at night to work without interruption. I attached electrodes to the back of my head (occipital lobes) and routed them through the amplifier to the inputs of an Ampex tape recorder and out to a loudspeaker. Alpha waves are mono. At first I couldn't distinguish what was noise and what was alpha. I watched the VU meters on the tape recorder. Alpha waves pulse from 8 to 12 cycles per second fairly regularly but in uneven bursts. They slow down and speed up a little, get louder and softer. Electrical noise is more complex and constant. Pretty soon I felt I was producing alpha. One is supposed to get into a relaxed, meditative state to unblock it but I learned to do so with relative ease.

Several of my colleagues suggested that I record the alpha waves on tape and subject them to manipulation in an electronic music studio. I quickly rejected that idea. Splicing alpha waves would have seemed like brain surgery. Anyway, it seemed to me that a live performance was much more interesting. A single person sitting in front of an audience with electrodes on his head, eyes closed, was more theatrically exciting than simply listening to sounds emanating from a loudspeaker.

As I was working with producing alpha waves I was struck by the size of the excursions of the loudspeaker cones. This was the period of development of the acoustic suspension loudspeaker by KLH and AR in nearby Cambridge. The excursions of the loudspeaker cones reminded me of pistons moving rapidly in and out. They looked as if they were moving a half an inch or more. I thought I could use the power of these signals to do work, to use the cone excursions as drummers that could play percussion instruments.

The night before the concert we set up sixteen percussion instruments: pairs of snare and bass drums, timpani, cymbals, and gongs, a piano with the lid open, a loudspeaker placed face down on the strings, a trash can and cardboard box, speakers placed inside. We distributed the instruments between the two floors of the Rose Art Museum. We placed loudspeakers near or touching each instrument so that when the bursts of alpha flowed out the instruments would resonate, each in its own way, and sound. The amplification system consisted of eight stereo home amplifiers cascaded in series. The output of one was routed to the input of the next and so on. The output of the Tektronix amp was simply routed into the first one. Throughout the course of the performance John simply panned the alpha waves to one of the sixteen loudspeakers in a more or less random manner. I suggested a ten-minute performance. Cage counter-suggested forty minutes! Forty minutes was a long time for a performance in those days. After the concert someone told me that one of my colleagues pretended to fall asleep while another gave him a hotfoot. (Some colleagues.)

Rozart Mix

Cage wrote me that he had an idea for a new piece but no time to work on it. The preparation would require the splicing of tape loops. Do you know what a tape loop is? There's little reason you would, we don't use them anymore. Everything is done with samplers nowadays. To make a loop you simply splice a length of tape together at both ends. Any sound recorded on the tape plays over and over again. Cage's proposed piece required at least twelve tape machines (the number of notes of the chromatic scale), amplified separately, and at least eighty-eight tape loops (the number of keys on the piano). It would require the services of at least four or maybe eight performers as loop-changers and tape recorder manipulators. The loops would be of greatly varying lengths. We would use mike stands for positioning the loops, some vertically, to look like a Jean Tinguely fountain. Cage asked me to have the letter photocopied—he had no carbon paper—and sent back to him. He wrote the notes about the splicing techniques in the margins of that letter and sent it back to me. He said we could record just anything, lots of speech, some music, not much in the way of continuous noises. The tape should be cut quite small—not more than four or five inches and down to tiny fragments. In the score he said to splice ignorantly, that is, not knowing what sounds were on the tape. He drew arrows at various angles to give an idea of how the splices should be cut. We were not to splice just forward and backward but at various angles in order to give sounds different attacks. A long angled splice would produce a gradual attack, a sharp cut, an abrupt one. We were actually shaping the sounds with our splices. We ended up with glorious noises. John said that if a splice should break, the repair job should take precedence over the other activities, but once a splice is repaired, the loop is to be exchanged for a new one. Among the necessary materials he mentioned something called splicing powder. I have no idea what he meant by that. I have asked around and no one else seems to know either. Earle Brown thought that it was used to keep the fingers dry while touching so much adhesive tape. I wrote him back with final details of the concert. Several months later, our correspondence was published by Peters Edition. The letters are the score of the piece. He called the piece *Rozart Mix*. (Rozart, Mozart, get it?)

We performed *Rozart Mix* several years ago in Crowell Hall at Wesleyan with about thirty-five students. The students went out and recorded sounds and came back with miles of tape. We spent weeks splicing loops, some a fraction of an inch long. We wanted a couple of loops to run up the length of the hall so we spliced about two hundred feet of tape in order to get a loop a hundred feet long. (I may be exaggerating.) We simply followed Cage's directions. It was a lot of hard work. We spliced day and night. It was wonderful. Chris Schiff, a graduate student composer, was in charge of splicing. During the performance he sat at a small table on stage with a splicing block, adhesive splicing tape and one-sided razor blades. He would repair loops that broke, then put them away to be used at a later time. The putting aside of repaired tape loops in *Rozart Mix* reminded me of discarding yarrow stalks in consulting the *I Ching*.

Motor Vehicle Sundown (Event)

I suggested we do George Brecht's *Motor Vehicle Sundown (Event)* (1960). You get a number of automobiles together and make sounds with them. You turn the lights and windshield wipers on and off, blow the horn, open and close the doors, and so forth. It's beautiful. All over America, cars drive up to A & W Root Beer stands and Dairy Queens at dusk. It's an American custom to gather this way. It reminds me of the circles wagon trains made in the West. I took a bicycle trip last summer up to the White Mountains and had to stop to eat wherever I could. I remembering sitting at a picnic table at the Lone Oak Drive-in in North Rochester, New Hampshire, watching families in cars and pickup trucks pull up and order hamburgers, hot dogs, and fried clams. Doors would open and slam shut, motors start up, a horn would sound inadvertently. I suddenly realized: "Hey, I'm in the middle of a performance of George Brecht's *Motor Vehicle Sundown (Event)*!"

We didn't actually perform the Brecht piece on the concert, but John was so elated by the performance of *Rozart Mix* he pretended to push cars away as they departed from the front of the museum.

7

CAGE AND TUDOR

Cartridge Music

Does anyone have a toothpick? This is the question I usually ask when I talk about John Cage's *Cartridge Music* (1960). Most people think of a toothpick as a trivial thing but in fact it is rather a sophisticated manufactured object. Here is a description from a toothpick manufacturer:

> A toothpick of essentially triangular cross section and tapered at both ends, one or both of the apex edge and base face thereof having an outwardly curved contour. A process for manufacturing said toothpicks involving forming V-shaped grooves of the requisite shape in a raw material and separating the toothpicks therefrom. A conventional type of toothpick made of wood and having a substantially triangular cross-section is marketed in strip form with toothpicks arranged parallel to the sides of one another as a connected unit, so that they can be broken off therefrom singly as required. The individual toothpicks are wedge-shaped and are manufactured in the form of a correspondingly wedge-shaped board, a flat end surface of the latter and a flat bottom side both being partly broken through by V-shaped grooves, extending in a straight line, which are formed in the upper side in a suitable manner.

Crazy as it may seem, with so many people in this class, we perform Cage's *Cartridge Music*. Does anyone know what a phonograph cartridge is? Or are they a thing of the past? The old LP or 78 record players had magnetic cartridges with phonograph needles in them. The needle would track the grooves on the record and transform the mechanical energy into electrical energy. For many years Cage had wanted to be able to hear small sounds and the sounds of physical objects. He was also looking for ways to make electronic music live. All one has to do is remove the needle in a phono cartridge and insert something else, a toothpick, for example. Twang the toothpick and you get the sound of wood. One can do the same thing with a pipe cleaner or a Slinky. The cartridge amplifies these objects enormously. We used to buy them at Radio Shack for about $2.98. They're hard to get nowadays, the phonograph record is virtually obsolete except for aficionados and disk jockeys. But we can substitute piezo disks, which work almost as well. A piezo disk is simply an audio transducer that transforms pressure into an electrical signal. It's about as large as a dime.

One of the reasons that Cage's music is so popular is that he is not afraid of whimsy. Toothpicks are unlikely objects to use in a musical performance but they are exquisitely engineered objects nonetheless. Slinkies are silly children's toys capable of stepping down a stairway, making hyper-reverberant sounds. They are really metal coils similar to the spring reverberation units we had in the old days and are still available in some rock-and-roll guitar amplifiers. That doubleness, that confusion as to function—one object put to a use it wasn't designed for—has a certain haiku quality. In haiku poetry often the mind has to travel a long distance to get from one image to another of two disparate images (ideas). This juxtaposition activates the mind and gives deep meaning as one listens to Cage's music. In one of his lectures Bob Wilson remarked that a baroque candelabra on a baroque table means one thing; a baroque candelabra on a rock in a meadow, for example, means something completely different.

The score of *Cartridge Music* consists of a page of instructions, as well as four transparent sheets—one with points, one with circles, another with a circle that looks like a clock face, and a fourth with a dotted curved line with a circle at the end of it—and twenty pieces of white paper with shapes on them. I don't know how Cage made these shapes but the twenty sheets have a corresponding number of shapes on them, from one to twenty. If one player plays the work, he or she uses the sheet with one shape on it; two players use the sheet with two shapes and so on. The first thing you do is to superimpose the transparencies over the sheet with shapes to get a determination for playing. You may place the sheets randomly, one on top of the other, only making sure that the circle at the end of the dotted line contains a point outside a shape and that the dotted line intersects at least one point within a shape. Where a dotted line intersects a point within a shape you produce a sound corresponding to that shape. What Cage means here is somewhat vague. I think he means that you make a sound with the object related to that particular shape, but to tell you the truth I have often simply traced the shape to help me move my object around to make sounds. That is not too different from Cage's practice of tracing stones with pencils in order to get melodic lines in pieces such as *Ryoanji*, for example. Intersection of the dotted line with a point outside the shape indicates auxiliary sounds made by any means other than those made by the objects in the cartridges. Cage often uses auxiliary sounds to interrupt the flow of an otherwise smooth and beautiful piece. You could amplify nearby microphone stands with contact microphones, for example. The intersections of the dotted lines with a circle within and outside a shape may be used to alter dynamic levels and tone controls respectively. In addition when a circle is intersected by both a boundary of a shape and the dotted line, a change of object is indicated.

The dotted line may intersect the clock face at various points. The clock face is measured in five-second segments. Where it enters will be your starting time. Where it exits is your ending time. You simply play for as long as your time in the clock says in

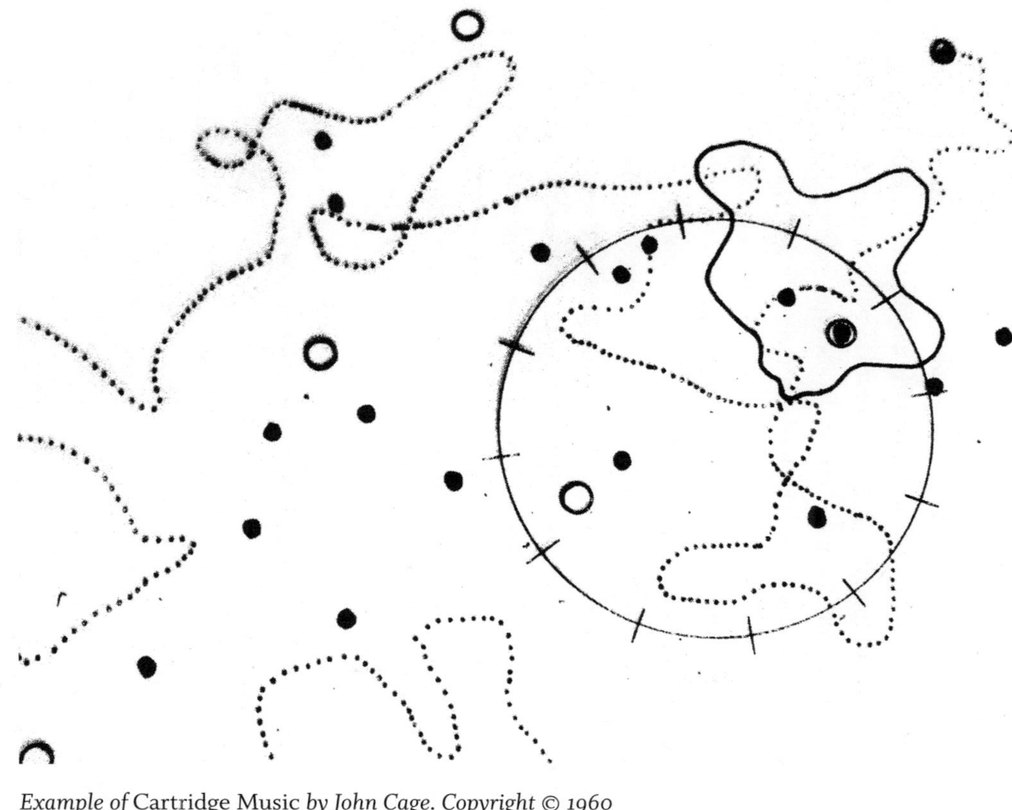

Example of Cartridge Music *by John Cage. Copyright © 1960 by C. F. Peters Corporation. Used by permission.*

relation to the chosen length of the performance. You may keep track of time any way you want. You could notate in some way when you enter and leave the circle or trace the clock face itself, showing where the lines enter and exit. Or you could trace the clock face, showing with arrows, for example, when you enter and exit. You have to make your own scores. You play only the segment of the dotted line that falls within the clock unless, of course, your line does not either enter or exit the clock face; then no specific time is given. You are in a no-time zone.

When a dotted line curls back on itself, it becomes a loop indicating the repetition of a sound an indefinite number of times. It isn't an opportunity to make banal rhythms.

Any number of players decides on a time length for a performance. For a three-minute performance you could superimpose the transparencies and the sheet with shapes three times to get three separate readings of a minute each. It doesn't really matter what order they are in, or what is the top or bottom, you'll get valid results. It sounds abstract, but it becomes clearer as you read through the score. Performing *Cartridge Music* will teach you how to follow a set of instructions that absolves you from having subjective input. This is very much in line with Cage's aesthetic. He doesn't care whether external sounds enter into the performance, either. Feedback, hum or any other electronic noise of any kind is welcome.

If you find yourself in a difficult situation simply find a way out. Cage suggests that, in cases where one or more readings are ambiguous, take both or neither of the readings. You've got four transparencies, twenty sheets of paper and a set of instructions that are a little vague. Cage doesn't want you to improvise. He doesn't want you to rely on memory and habit. If you were improvising, you might not choose the proportions that the lines and shapes offer you, particularly the silences that might happen to be longer than playing time. If we perform *Cartridge Music* accurately we'll directly experience the lovely and unexpected proportions that chance gives us.

Toneburst

I was on a panel with David Tudor in Munich several years ago, and he started talking about John Cage. I rebuked him gently and suggested he talk about himself for a change. I reminded him that he invented the table of electronics that saved our lives in the Sixties. At that time it was almost inconceivable that the Boston Symphony, for example, would ever play a piece of ours. We were dead as artists in that context. It might take you a year or more to write a symphony, you'd copy out all the parts, then, if you were very lucky, an orchestra might decide to play your piece. It might be played again, and that was it. It was a dead end. We composers were in a cultural war. We were colonized by the European musical establishment. Things are better nowadays.

Then David Tudor came along. You would attend one of his concerts and notice a table filled with homemade electronic devices housed in plastic soap dishes. They reminded me of summer camp. They were amazing; there'd be input and output jacks. You wouldn't know what was in them. They would process sound and make this electronic music. David made his own orchestra out of these, each one plugged into the other in a complex web. He would buy all the components cheaply at Radio Shack, things he found and picked up. He really saved our lives. He enabled us to make our own work. A bunch of people would meet, get together, make these pieces, and play them. We just sidestepped the huge classical music institutions.

John Cage and David Tudor always thought that live performance was more interesting than hearing taped music coming out of loudspeakers. Works such as Cage's *Rozart Mix*, which consists of miles of recorded tape, is nonetheless performed live.

When David sat at his table of electronics, there was no need for him to make any unwarranted gestures because the sounds were all in the circuitry. He didn't have to make them. When sounds are made on a piano, you can see the player making them. But if the sounds (signals) are in the electronics, as they are in *Toneburst* (1974), for example, David would be sitting there doing mysterious things. Sometimes he would turn a dial and nothing would happen. Or something would happen at a time lag. It was wonderful to go to concerts where somebody was doing something different than standing up and showing off. You were watching a wonderful musician paying more attention to the sounds as they were happening than making them happen. It's a strange idea, listening more than actually doing. Neely Bruce recently mentioned having gone to a tape music concert of historic European electronic music, composed mostly in the Fifties and Sixties. He remarked how appropriate that means of performance was, presenting works on tape. The composers were interested in control, they wanted the end product to be fixed. I remember going to tape music concerts where the lights went down and the sounds came out of speakers, and you imagined you were in the mind of the composer. I just bought a CD of Bach's *Mass in B Minor*. I listen to it at home and it doesn't bother me that I'm not watching a conductor and the chorus and the instruments. It's rather wonderful, in fact; you don't have to watch one more egotistic conductor. I would rather go to a concert, but you can't go to concerts all the time. It's wonderful to play music at home, isn't it? I don't know why I'm explaining this to you.

So, we're still involved in the beginnings of live electronic music. On Sunday after the concert we went over to see the installation in the gallery of *Toneburst*, and I was trying to figure out what those scores on the wall had to do with the sound. Sophia Ogielska, a friend of David's, had made visual representations of David's circuits. David Behrman said that Tudor was secretive about his circuitry. Even a couple of months before he died, he kept much of that information to himself. What was in his boxes? We both agreed that wasn't such a hot idea, because then where would the music go from there? Very few people can play it. I remember talking with Steve Reich about this. I had been in Australia, and I visited the Percy Grainger museum in Melbourne. Grainger was an Australian composer who made a name for himself by orchestrating English folk tunes. That was his day job. On the other hand he made experiments using electronics, and even built eccentric devices that played his works. They don't work anymore; they can't be played by anybody. Steve Reich said he didn't think that was smart, because you end up with museum pieces, dinosaurs that can't be played and don't flow in the mainstream. That's a problem with this kind of work. When you hear a David Tudor work, you're at a loss to know what's going on, whereas if you look at a score of a Beethoven symphony, you can re-create it more or less the way it was originally done.

Another problem was learning electronics. We weren't trained to do that. I didn't know anything about electronics. I'm not good with soldering; I can barely read a circuit diagram. For those people who had a knack for it, live electronics was a very exciting and valuable thing. I remember that Tudor said on that panel that he had asked Stockhausen, "Why don't you learn how to make your own electronics?" Stockhausen replied, "Industry will provide me with what I need." That didn't happen. Industry didn't provide us with what we needed. Industry made synthesizers popular enough to sell in the hundreds of thousands.

From the very beginning, we weren't interested in mass-produced synthesizers because they were made to imitate musical instruments. They were made to plug a guitar into and make the sound interesting. So certain composers started making circuits for specific works. If you go to *Toneburst* over in the Zilkha Gallery the circuit diagrams give you an idea of the flow of the sounds, which is what a classical musical score does. You read a

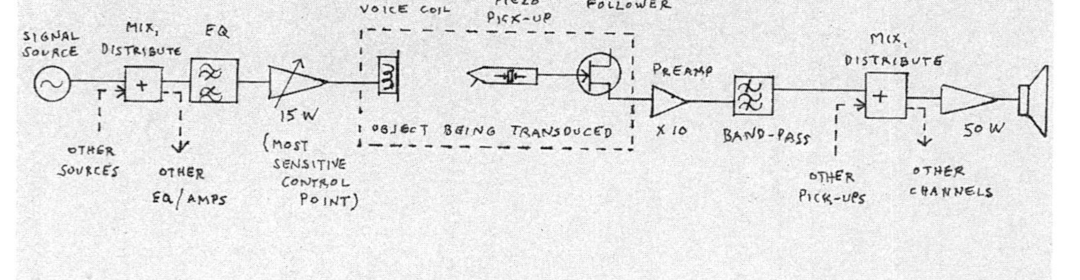

David Tudor, generalized electronic circuitry diagram for Rainforest (4), *1973. Used by permission of the David Tudor Trust. Image courtesy of the Getty Research Institute, Los Angeles (980039).*

Beethoven symphony score from left to right. David's circuit diagrams give you an idea of how the sounds—signals—are routed. The circuit became the score. You can see the one for *Rainforest (4)* in the accompanying illustration.

4′ 33″

Let's talk about the "silent piece." It's one of those works that everyone talks about but few really know. But as Wesleyan students, you are going to know what the silent piece is. It may not be the most important thing in your education, but I want to make sure that you don't just know it from hearsay. This work is in three movements. Very classical: The Father, Son, and the Holy Ghost; the Three Graces; one, two, three. Each movement is marked tacet (not *tacit*). *Tacet* (from the Latin) is a musical term used when an instrument in an orchestra is silent during an entire movement. Say you have a four-movement symphony. Usually the ketledrums don't play in the slow movement. So instead of writing out pages of empty measures, the composer simply writes tacet.

Actually, Cage made an earlier spatially notated version of *4′ 33″* (1952). It consists of blank pages divided by vertical lines down the length of the pages, spatially indicating the timings. For publication he decided to make a more conventional score using the term tacet, which is easily understood by most musicians.

The total length of its first performance was four minutes and thirty-three seconds. Guess where it was played? Woodstock! Several years ago I was on a television program created by video artist Nam June Paik, called *Who Is John Cage?* He wanted me to be the college professor who lectures authoritatively on Cage. I was in a funny mood that day and said that the real Woodstock, not the rock-and-roll festival with thousands of people wallowing in the mud—that wasn't really important—but the Woodstock of August 29, 1952, when John Cage's *4′ 33″* was played for an audience of about ten people—that was the real Woodstock. I was kidding. I wouldn't say that now.

The three movements were timed: 33″, 2′ 40″, and 1′ 20″. It has long been a question as to how these timings were arrived at. There is good evidence that Cage used methods he invented for his great piano work, *Music of Changes* (1951). *4′ 33″* was performed by David Tudor, who indicated the beginnings and endings of the movements by closing and opening the lid of the keyboard. The work, however, may be performed by any instrumentalist or combination of instrumentalists, for any length of time. It was performed in Harvard Square in the early Seventies by several performers for an entire day. It was beautiful, watching a concentrating performer sitting at a grand piano in the middle of bustling Harvard Square. The published score has specific timings, but Cage branched it out into a more general idea. You do that often in conceptual works, that is, works in which the idea is the work itself. You make a specific performance plan so that somebody who wants to perform it that way may do so. Then you generalize the idea so that it ramifies into other versions.

4′ 33″ is a work in which no purposeful sounds are made. If no purposeful sounds are made, what constitutes the work? It's the showing of time and focusing attention on the sounds of the environment. Where does that occur in another culture? It reminds one of a Japanese rock garden, where there's very little to see except raked sand and carefully placed stones. The changing seasons, the angle of the sun, the moon, light, darkness, everything in the environment comes into the garden. It's forever changing. So instead of making a garden where the plantings and flowers are exactly schematized, as in the formal gardens in eighteenth-century Europe, for example, the Japanese rock garden is virtually empty. But it's filled with the changing environment. The viewer pays attention to nature.

Most performers play it the way David Tudor played it. They want to be historically accurate. He used a stopwatch because the timings are very important. *4′ 33″*—the "silent piece"—has been recorded by Gianni-Emilio Simonetti on Cramps Records in Italy. You can hear the sound of the piano lid being opened and closed as well as the record noise.

4′ 33″ is beneficial to perform every once in a while. It makes you pay attention to the sounds around you. Any external sound is a nuisance if you're trying to communicate. But if you quiet yourself and listen, then it may become a wonderful presence and it's not a nuisance anymore. Even someone coughing may become a part of this piece. It's wonderful to learn to accept the sounds of the environment, about which you can't do anything anyway. The "silent piece" is a one-of-a-kind work that raises a lot of questions. I hope you all understand it. It's simple, but simple things often get misunderstood.

There's a wonderful story about the first performance: someone drove his automobile into the concert hall and left the motor on. I don't think it's true but let's pretend it is.

Ryoanji

Ryoanji is a rock garden in Kyoto that John Cage visited years ago. Fifteen stones are placed on raked sand. Some scholars insist the rocks were placed in a specific pattern. Cage asserts that they were randomly positioned. Anyway they were placed there a long time ago. There's no vegetation, only carefully raked sand. There's a wall on the opposite side of the garden that's been weathered by time. It looks as if oil has oozed out of the stones. The moss-like pattern was made by nature and is as beautiful as any pattern anyone has ever made. Visitors come to this rock garden and simply sit and look. Viewing it is supposed to put you in a peaceful state of mind. As you view the garden your consciousness changes. Your feelings are those of peace and meditation and quiet. That is something that Cage tried to get for a long time during his life—works that didn't evoke feelings of anger or joy, but a quiet acceptance of life, even its vicissitudes. I suppose we're talking about Zen.

Years later, after visiting Ryoanji, he made a series of pieces called *Ryoanji* (1983–1985) for various instruments, including flute, oboe, trombone, double bass, and voice. The notation consists mostly of slides, glissandos. I remember Cage remarking how surprised he was to discover that the oboe was capable of sliding although through a fairly narrow range. One thinks of the oboe as a rigid instrument. It is so accurate in sounding the note A for the instruments of the orchestra to tune up to. Cage collected fifteen stones and traced their shapes with a pencil on music paper. He said that the five line staves were the "area of the garden." He didn't trace the stones directly, but drew the shapes on paper as templates to ensure that repetitions would occur. He said he couldn't count on the accuracy of tracing the stones directly.

There's a percussion part, too. The player is instructed to make two sounds simultaneously, each on a different material. Cage doesn't want them to be too resonant, either, because he wants them to sound like sounds of nature, not like high-tech percussion instruments. The score consists of single sounds separated by one, two, or three rests. So there's steady but uneven beat; you feel an ictus that is stable and unpredictable at the same time. Cage says it's supposed to represent raked sand. He says that the percussionist should make imperceptible changes in loudness, as though the light on the stones is changing. So this performance consists of sharp, short sounds, surrounded by silences and beautiful curved shapes that are the tracings of stones. What a beautiful idea! For some reason this music seems to exist out of time. It's difficult to place it.

A few years ago I attended a performance of *Ryoanji* by the S. E. M. Ensemble at the Paula Cooper Gallery in New York. Several players were placed around the room. Each one played freely and unsynchronized. There was a lot of silence. One had a feeling of spaciousness and calm. It was uncanny.

I just read in the *Campus Report* that the Mansfield Freeman

East Asian Center has just opened a Japanese rock garden. It's on Washington Terrace. They've built a tearoom and a beautiful Japanese rock garden with raked sand. It behooves us all, since we listened to *Ryoanji*, to go over and visit it. It connects with Cage's ideas and would be a beautiful thing for us to do. Perhaps someone will perform *Ryoanji* there sometime.

8

SONIC ARTS UNION

Wolfman

In 1966 Robert Ashley, David Behrman, Gordon Mumma, and I formed The Sonic Arts Union. I first met Bob and Gordon at the Feldman-Brown Concert in 1963. They had driven down to New York from Ann Arbor. Gordon and Bob lived in Ann Arbor and were part of a different musical culture. Often I didn't quite understand what they were talking about. The two of them had founded an independent electronic music studio in Ann Arbor. It had nothing to do with the University of Michigan Department of Music, even though they had been there as students. They got a hold of a couple of tape recorders and invited composers from all over the country to come and make electronic music.

Bob was interested in speech; he had worked in the language lab at the University of Michigan and learned a great deal about the formation of speech, as well as psychoacoustics. Gordon played the French horn, a skill he maintained throughout several works with electronics. David lived in New York. I had met him earlier through Christian Wolff at Harvard, later in the early Sixties at Darmstadt where I heard his early work, *Canons*, for piano (David Tudor) and percussion (Christoph Caskell). We were all trained in music, not in science or electronics, but when electronic music became a necessity, Gordon and David were inspired enough to learn electronic circuitry by themselves. I had been involved in a concert in New York a few years earlier, organized by Ben Paterson and Philip Corner under the name Sonic Arts Group, so I suggested we simply steal that name. It was just a name on a program. So we called ourselves the Sonic Arts Group.

We weren't really a group, however. We didn't improvise, we didn't collaborate. We simply shared equipment and played in each other's pieces. One night, Bob called me and said he'd changed the name to Sonic Arts Union. He didn't like the name Sonic Arts Group because people called us SAG. Bob hated silly acronyms. I agreed. We never met and argued about anything; if one of us decided something, it was fine with the rest of us. So we became the Sonic Arts Union. SAU sounded awkward, but at least it wasn't SAG. The Beatles, The Rolling Stones, and REM were good names.

One of the signature works of the early Sixties was Robert Ashley's *Wolfman* (1964) for amplified voice and tape. It was the loudest piece of music anyone had heard at that time. I suppose you could say that it was the reverse side of Feldman's coin. Morty's sounds are so soft you have to lean toward the performers to hear what's going on. Sometimes you wonder if you are hearing all of them. In *Wolfman* you lean back and let them come to you. The sounds are so powerful that you are in a continual state of analysis, your mind constantly moves in an effort to isolate the minutest details. Ashley is a close-up, Feldman, a long shot. Or perhaps it is the other way around. You have to lean into Feldman's softness but you instinctively back away from Ashley's loudness. It's the difference between a microscope and a telescope.

Throughout the piece the volume level is turned up so high that feedback is created between a microphone and loudspeakers positioned around the hall. If left unattended feedback grows and grows to unbearable levels. The British call it "howl-round." There are several ways to control feedback: one is to use a compressor/limiter, an audio circuit designed to limit abrupt sound spikes while recording, so as not to get distortion. Another is to shift the pitch of the feedback slightly so that there is no steady tone to continually reinforce itself. Nicolas Collins does that in his work *Pea*

Soup. He uses a phase shifter that slightly shifts the pitch of feedback strands in an installation environment. Because the pitch of the feedback is continually changing, even by extremely small increments, the feedback, which relies on a single sustained pitch for its buildup, cannot establish itself. A third way is to introduce a sound into the loop between the microphone and loudspeaker. This is what Ashley does in *Wolfman*. He "sings" into a microphone positioned close to his mouth. In a prose score he gives four components that the performer varies during the performance: pitch, loudness, vowel, and closure. The vowel is changed by moving the tongue from the front to the back of the mouth, thereby changing the size of the oral cavity. As he does so, a range of vowels is produced, from *i* (long) to *h* (deep and heavily aspirated). By closure Bob means a continuum between jaws closed with lips pursed to jaw open with lips drawn as far as possible. What he is actually doing is coupling—a small room of variable size (the human mouth) changes to a large one of fixed size (the concert hall). What an idea!

Bob wrote out a set of instructions to guide the performer in moving through these parameters. In order to manage the four components he invented a simple process of controlled improvisation. You could start at any point, then gradually vary one of the four parameters while keeping the other three constant. Then you would alter a second parameter, keeping the other three constant. You couldn't change any of the variables until the three others had been changed. This produced an evolving structure that was always moving ahead. It was a simple and effective way of preventing crescendos and diminuendos, risings up and fallings back, and other banal gestures that improvisers are prone to rely on.

Because the microphone is so close to the performer's mouth it takes only the slightest effort by the performer to effect an enormous change. This gives the work a great sense of irony. Soft sounds control loud sounds. You are watching what looks like a performer screaming into a microphone when actually he is barely making a sound. *Wolfman* is an homage to amplification. Bob used to perform that piece so loudly listeners would leave the concert hall. They were not accustomed to hearing such loud sounds. Often, the concert sponsors or sound technicians would complain that the volume was so high the speakers would be damaged (as if Bob didn't know enough about loudspeaker capability). They would try to lower the levels. Actually Bob had a precise idea about the volume: he required one half watt of power per person in the audience.

Performances of *Wolfman* had a sinister aspect to them. Bob used to stage them as if they were a nightclub performance, his face close to the mike, lit by a spotlight. Sometimes he would put a light directly under his chin, pointing up, so that his face would be luridly transfigured. It was frightening. The theatricality, however, was a decoy masking the true identity of the work. *Wolfman* was really a study in amplification and resonance.

People sometimes thought that their ears were getting hurt, but that was more psychological than physical. Bob used to say it was like ballroom dancing. If your partner liked you, she wouldn't feel uncomfortable if you squeezed her. But if she didn't like you, she would say it hurt. I never felt uncomfortable performing or listening to *Wolfman*. One of the experiences of listening was riding the threshold of loudness. You would constantly examine whether or not the sounds were loud enough to hurt you (they never were). At what point would they simply be too loud to bear? There was something exhilarating about that.

Bob had created two tapes to accompany the performance: *Wolfman*, about six minutes' duration, and *The Fourth of July*, about eighteen minutes long. For the *Fourth of July* Bob recorded the sounds of a neighbor's backyard picnic with a parabolic microphone. The chief characteristic of a parabola is that a wave of any kind that strikes any point on its surface is reflected to a central focal point. A mike placed at that point will receive multiples of the same signal from all the points of reflection. The FBI uses parabolic mikes for eavesdropping and to pick out individual speakers in a crowd. They are also used to pick up quarterbacks calling signals in football games and individual birds in bird recording.

Hornpipe

Hornpipe (1967) is a milestone of experimental music. You can understand why Gordon Mumma would call it *Hornpipe* since he played the French horn. The term also refers to a popular dance form in the seventeenth century. Gordon had designed a box of electronics he called the Cybersonic Console. Cybernetics was a branch of engineering pioneered by Norbert Wiener of MIT. It refers to self-regulating systems. The Balinese irrigate their rice fields using bamboo pipes, which, as they fill up with water, become unbalanced. This causes them to spill their contents into the next pool of water, so as to combat flooding. When the pipe is empty, it rocks back to its original position and starts filling up again.

Gordon would walk out on stage with his French horn, wearing his Console on his belt. It consisted of a microphone and eight variable resonance circuits. He designed and built it himself. He was the only person who knew exactly how it worked. The microphone was inserted into the bell of the horn and would listen to what was happening in the room. Gordon would play sounds into the room, the microphone would pick them up and the Console would do an analysis of the room's acoustics. Depending on how he set the parameters on the Console, it would respond to the acoustical situation. It contained a bank of filters. *Hornpipe* was one of the first musical works that used acoustical testing of an environment as a formal structure for music.

Music of a given time and period is made for the spaces in which it's played. Chamber music, usually performed in small, dry rooms, may have a complexity that works composed for larger spaces may not have. A typical reverberation time for a large concert hall is about two seconds. Opera houses have shorter times, for the sake of the clarity of understanding the words. Any conductor knows that there is no absolute tempo at which a work should move. So much depends on the reverberation time of the space. One may rehearse a Bach cantata at one set of tempos, then have to slow them down or speed them up in performance. Reflective surfaces surround a performance of a Beethoven symphony, but Beethoven's intention was not to articulate the space; it had to do with all the musical things we are well acquainted with.

Sometimes Gordon would substitute an oboe (double) reed for the normal French horn mouthpiece, turning that mellow brass sound into a raucous shawm-like instrument. The reeds vibrate against one another, producing that rich, grainy medieval oboe sound. Gordon loves abrasive sounds. Perhaps abrasive is a bad adjective; instead let's say rich or complex. He worked with electronics so much he learned to love these complex sound aggregates. He always chose the most extreme sounds to put in, and made no attempt to make them beautiful. The climax of the work occurs when the system becomes saturated and unstable and the electronic sounds kick in. The composer/performer doesn't determine when this happens, the circuitry does. It's a magical moment.

Dresden Interleaf

Right away the title *Dresden Interleaf* reminds one of the firebombing of Dresden, Germany, on February 13, 1945. World War II in Europe was virtually over. The English and the Americans decided to punish the Germans by devising a pattern of saturation bombing of the city of Dresden. They also wanted to learn something about bombing, if you can imagine that. They divided the city of Dresden into a grid and sent twelve hundred airplanes over, dropping incendiary bombs, and for two days covered every square inch of the city, methodically and geometrically. They destroyed the whole city. They didn't need to do it, the war was already won. It was a cold-blooded exercise in warfare. Gordon Mumma's *Dresden Interleaf* is meant to be played between any other two pieces, as a sort of disruption.

Dresden Interleaf is a tape collage composition made of found material, including a choral fragment from Mendelssohn's *Reformation Symphony*. (The "Dresden Amen" is played in the first movement and referenced in the third.) There's also a sound track from a World War II movie, in which aircraft pilots are talking to one another during a bombing mission. In live performances Gordon used model airplane engines as part of the sound material. He'd start them up and they'd make that raucous sputtering noise. You could see the smoke and smell the gasoline. It was wonderful. *Dresden Interleaf* is classical electronic music from the Sixties; you can't make these sounds with a synthesizer. They're analog sounds made by hours of recording, splicing, and overdubbing with homemade equipment.

Mesa

Mesa is a large-scale work for bandoneon and electronics by Gordon Mumma. It was commissioned by the Merce Cunningham Dance Company for their dance, *Place*, and was written for David Tudor.

The bandoneon is a type of Argentine accordion made popular by tango composer Astor Piazzolla. It was invented in the early nineteenth century by German inventor Heinrich Band, who intended it to be used in folk music and religious services. Immigrants and sailors brought it to Argentina in the late nineteenth century. It is similar to the piano accordion but has buttons on both sides of the instrument rather than keys on a keyboard. On some bandoneons the buttons in their "out" position have different pitches than in their "in" position. This makes it devilishly difficult to play but it was right up David Tudor's alley.

Gordon routed the sounds of the bandoneon to his Cybersonic Console, which extended the dynamic range of the instrument and shifted the pitches enharmonically, creating the raucous timbres that Gordon loved so much. The stereo characteristics of the bandoneon—the right and left sides of the instruments are separate—were expanded into a quadraphonic soundscape. Different parts of the timbral spectra are heard in different channels of the quadraphonic playback.

The salient characteristic of *Mesa* is instantaneous change in loudness. Such extreme abruptness was hardly ever experienced in music before, except in some of Karlheinz Stockhausen's piano pieces (*Klavierstücke*) in which the dynamic contrasts are so extreme and abrupt that David Tudor's first recordings were unacceptable because of print-through. Print-through is caused by the bleeding of a signal to adjacent layers of tape, as it is stored on its reel. It is heard as a backward and forward pre-echo and is therefore unusable.

The title refers to the geological formation of mesas, table-shaped mountains vertical on their sides and flat on top. It also relates to the monolithic structure of certain semiconductors (mesa diodes?) used in electronic circuitry of the time. (Coincidentally, the abrupt on–sustain–off characteristics of *Mesa* relates in a way to the plateau dynamics of the baroque era.) Gordon made a special version for the Sonic Arts Union by substituting harmonicas (mouth organs) for bandoneons, keeping the reedy quality of the original sound material.

Runthrough

David Behrman's *Runthrough* (1967–1968) is an improvisation for four players. Two players work dials and switches that control various sound generators and modulators while the other two shine small flashlights onto photo resistors housed in tin cans, distributing sounds to four loudspeakers deployed around the concert space. A photo resistor, the kind that will cause an alarm to go off if an intruder breaks a beam of light, is simply a semiconductor which, when illuminated, drops in resistance. The photo resistors were housed in Campbell Soup cans. Each player would rotate a small flashlight into a tin can, spinning the sounds at various speeds around the space. Two players control the placement of the sounds, the other two had control of the sounds themselves. David designed and built his own configuration of homemade components, all of which could be found in commercially available synthesizers at the time, including sine, pulse, and ramp wave oscillators, voltage control amplifiers, and ring modulators. David's system is designed for a specific work, not as a common denominator of what a large consumer public wanted. It sounds better than store-bought synthesizers. It has the mark of a master craftsman.

Sine waves are pure, without overtones; pulse waves are complex, their timbre varies depending on how long their duty cycle or "on" portion is relative to its complete cycle. When it is on half the time, it is called a square wave and consists of all odd-numbered overtones or harmonics. The nomenclature of these wave forms is derived from the shapes they assume when viewed on an oscilloscope, a device consisting of a cathode ray tube and fluorescent screen—the vertical axis representing the amplitude (loudness) of the signal, the horizontal, the frequency (pitch). A voltage control amplifier is simply an amplifier that can be controlled by an external signal. A ring modulator produces the sums and differences of two or more frequencies fed into its input while suppressing the original signals. It was simple to make; its name is derived from the ring-like arrangement of its four diodes.

The most exciting possibility that voltage control offered the composer was that virtually every component could be used as a sound source and a control signal. One of the salient characteristics of *Runthrough*—slow crescendos followed by thumps of sound—was generated by ramp waves controlling voltage control amplifiers. A ramp wave, also known as a sawtooth wave, rises from zero to a pre-determined level, then falls abruptly to zero again. In the audio range its timbre consists of all the overtones above the fundamental frequency, decreasing in loudness the higher up you go. When tuned below audibility, that is, too low to be heard as sounds by the human ear, it may be used as a control voltage, imparting its envelope (shape) to whatever components it is patched into.

One of the characteristics of electronic music is that it is steady state; once it's turned on it stays on. With wind or brass instruments, for example, you only have a certain amount of air, so there have to be short silences between sounds, to allow players to breathe. String players have to change bow every few seconds causing very short silences that are mitigated by playing legato (smoothly). And so, conventional music is made of melodic and rhythmic material that stops and starts. With electronics it is seductive and natural to let these sounds change a little bit, stay on a long time, and fill up a space.

Runthrough has an all-over form, similar to Jackson Pollack's action paintings, that is, you hear everything there is to hear most of the time. Conceived as a quasi-improvised performance work, *Runthrough* allows ample time for the possibilities offered by his circuitry to unfold. There are, however, abrupt changes in rhythm, texture, and loudness that can only be achieved by the electronic medium. The circuit, amplifier, and loudspeaker are quicker than the bowed string or blown column of air. The only other work that matched and perhaps exceeded these quick shifts of level change was Gordon Mumma's *Mesa*, in which sustained planes of softness and loudness alternate instantaneously. Listening to a recording of *Runthrough* one is struck by how much of the acoustic space one can hear. This time-space, as well as the repetitive rhythmic figures that dominate the performance, served to articulate the acoustic characteristics of the space. (I imagine the vocalizations of thousands of tiny whales echoing off the walls of the room.) Listening to *Runthrough* is an exhilarating experience.

Wave Train

In 1998 the Wadsworth Athenaeum in Hartford asked me to give a talk about wave phenomena in conjunction with an exhibition of Lee Lozano's *Wave Paintings*. Lozano (1930–1999) had made a series of eleven large canvases each 96 inches high and 42 inches wide consisting of wavy lines of varying size, from two 48-inch waves to 192 half-inch ripples. She said they were a reference to the electromagnetic spectrum.

As I was thinking about what to talk about two other works from the Sixties immediately came to mind: Michael Snow's *Wavelength* and David Behrman's *Wave Train*. In Snow's film the camera moves closer and closer to a point between two windows on one wall of the room, finally focusing on a picture of ocean waves. The film is forty-five minutes long but seems to have been taken over a two or three-day time span. The movement toward the wall seems continuous but was actually filmed in steps. There was something about the purity and neutrality of waves and their motions that attracted certain artists who wanted to make nonsubjective and at the same time expressive works. There is a chapter in Italo Calvino's *Mr. Palomar*, in which the hero, sitting on a beach, muses on the transient nature of ocean waves. Where do they begin? Where do they end? How does one differentiate them?

In *Wave Train* David Behrman explores the resonant characteristics of a grand piano with feedback. Guitar microphones are placed in various locations on the strings of the piano; then the gains on the mikes' amplifiers are raised to the point of feedback, exciting the strings. The performer's job is to ride the feedback, raising and lowering the volume levels, creating arcs of sound waves. David likens this activity to surfing where one is constantly monitoring one's position along a surging wave front. From time to time, the mikes are repositioned (when the gains are down) to explore different parts of the piano.

Wave Songs

Instead of giving a lecture on wave phenomena I asked the Athenaeum if I could compose a work honoring Lozano's *Wave Paintings*. They agreed. I wrote *Wave Songs*, eleven solos for female voice with two pure wave oscillators. I took the proportions of the paintings as the basis of my musical miniatures. In each solo two oscillators are tuned relative to the size of the waves in the corresponding painting. Throughout the work the singer sings against the oscillator tones creating audible beats at speeds determined by the distances between the tones. Each painting is 96 inches high; each song lasts 96 seconds. In each painting the number of inches is divided by the size of the waves; in each solo the oscillators are tuned inversely to the size of the waves. For example, in the *Two-Wave Painting* each wave measures 48 inches (ninety-six divided by two). In the first solo the oscillators are tuned 48 cycles apart producing audible beats 48 times a second. In each succeeding solo the distance between the oscillator tones becomes narrower until, in *Solo XI*, corresponding to the *192-Wave Painting*, they are within a half a cycle of each other, producing one beat every two seconds. While the number of waves in Lozano's paintings increase as they get smaller, the number of beats in the solos decrease as the tunings get closer. The reason for this contrariness is because in order to imitate the *Two-Wave Painting*, for example, I would have had to tune the two oscillators over a minute and a half time span (one beat every 48 seconds), a tempo I thought to be too slow for human performance.

The Athenaeum kindly let me invite Joan La Barbara to come to Hartford to perform the piece. She performed it in the Matrix Gallery, a small exhibition space within the Athenaeum, surrounded by the eleven Lozano paintings. The artist had stipulated that the paintings be leaned up against the walls so that the texture of the paintings could be more physically perceived. I imagined the work as a mini opera with Joan taking the part of Lee Lozano, singing her paintings into existence or perhaps simply humming to herself as she worked on them.

It was extremely hot on the day of the performance. Shelly Casto of the Wadsworth was thoughtful enough to procure several hundred paper fans for the audience to cool themselves with during the performances. There was no air conditioning in the gallery. We soon discovered, however, that the fanning motion disturbed the sound waves. Pure (sine) waves, having no overtones, may be perceived physically particularly if the acoustics of the room are dry enough, that is, if they don't reflect too much sound. If you move around the room you can feel their presence. Even if you move a little, you can disturb them. It's like standing in a pool of water and sending out ripples with small movements of your body.

Unforeseen Events

Unforeseen Events (1991) is one of a long series of interactive computer pieces by David Behrman. Starting as far back as 1977 David has composed works for human performers and computer, upgrading his equipment as technological times change. *On the Other Ocean* and *Figure in a Clearing* utilized the rudimentary toy-like Kim-1 microcomputer. For these works David designed six pitch-sensing circuits that could remember the order and timing of pitches played into them through microphones. Two performers improvised on these pitches causing changes in harmonies stored in two homemade synthesizers.

In most of his pieces David collaborates with other musicians not so much out of shyness but from a firm belief in the artistic strength of such a way of working. In *Unforeseen Events* he collaborated with Ben Neill, who plays a modified trumpet that he developed in the mid-Eighties with the help of Robert Moog. It includes MIDI controllers that are connected directly to the computer.

Unforeseen Events is in four parts. In all of them the computer responds to trumpet calls, long tones, and single notes, creating harmonies, chords, and arpeggiated figures that sustain or change pitch and timbre in subtle ways. In Part Two, *Fishing for Complements*, the composer listens to what's going on and enters changes into the computer. In Part Three, *Witch Grass*, only when the performer pauses do the harmonies move away from their origins and don't stop until the performer plays again.

In all his works Behrman avoids the pitfall of many interactive works, that is, direct cause and effect, first cousin to call and response, a technique that appears in many world musics but sounds out of place in experimental music. Call and response is oppressive. Each player *must* respond to what is given by another. It's too predictable, too. It only works when something gets in the way between the call and its answer. As you listen to Behrman's pieces you only get glimmers of directness; most of the time the relationships are interrupted and distant and therefore engage the listener in tantalizing ways.

Years ago I went to India to collaborate with a group of Indian musicians. Before I left I recorded empty spaces at Wesleyan that I planned to playback in various performance spaces in India. The idea was to bring my spaces into theirs. I had recorded Crowell Hall in January. Because of the cold weather the windows expanded and contracted periodically making loud, sharp cracking sounds. The North Indian tabla player, having been trained in call and response, would invariably slap one of his drums following a sharp sound. It was absolutely predicable and useless for my purposes. As we were rehearsing Wesleyan English professor Joe Reed, who joined in our trip, came to the door of the space and looked in. I explained my predicament and asked for his advice. He immediately suggested that the drummer hit his drum *before* he heard a window crack. What a wonderful solution! Now we had unpredictability, anticipation, and the element of time. Something banal in music was turned on its head. Now you had response and call, which was much more interesting.

Vespers

In the late Sixties I was looking for something outside of music that would inspire me. I didn't want to write the kind of music that everyone else did. It didn't interest me to write for conventional musical instruments. It didn't even interest me to play an instrument, actually, although I was making a living as a choral conductor. I wanted to find my own idea. Virgil Thomson gave a lecture once in which he said, "What I demand from a composer is that he be original." The audience booed him. They didn't like the idea that a composer would think he or she had to be original.

I began to read *Listening in the Dark* by Donald Griffin, a pioneering work in echolocation. Griffin had also written a more popular book on this subject, *Echoes of Bats and Men*. It was a comprehensive study of the sound sending and receiving acuity of bats. Griffin discovered how bats avoid obstacles and hunt for food. He extended wires across his lab and observed how bats avoided hitting them. They were extremely skilled in doing this. Because sound waves have to be smaller than the objects they're bouncing off of, bats learned to emit trains of extremely high pulse waves, so high we humans can't hear them. Low sounds have longer wavelengths; they spread out, they can even go around corners. High sounds, with shorter wavelengths, are more directional. You can actually measure the wavelength of any musical sound. Here is a simple formula for doing so:

Wavelength = speed of sound (ca. 1130 feet/second)/frequency.

So A-natural at 440 cycles per second has a wavelength of about 2.6 ft.

When the echoes from a flying insect come back to the bat, it can tell how far away the insect is, where it is, and how fast it's moving. Griffin's book gave me a lot of ideas. I began thinking of sounds in terms of short and long wavelengths, not as high and low pitches or notes written in time from left to right on a page. I was truly impressed by these creatures that employ sound so exquisitely for survival.

There was an interesting program on television the other night. A young man has learned how to echolocate skillfully enough to negotiate through his neighborhood without bumping into things. He makes clicks by snapping his tongue against his palate. It was uncanny. He could tell you what every object was. It was the first time, I think, that a human being has learned how to echolocate.

It often happens that when you are looking for something and your mind is prepared sufficiently you find it almost as if by accident. I happened to meet a man in Cambridge, Massachusetts, who was working for a company called *Listening Incorporated*. The company was trying to develop ways of communicating with dolphins. They were manufacturing a device called a Sondol (sonar-dolphin), a hand-held pulse wave oscillator. You know what sonar does. You send out a sound wave, it reflects off an approaching ship, for example, bounces back and tells you how far away it is. Radar is similar but it employs radio waves. I borrowed a prototype of a Sondol and turned it on. I adjusted the pulse rate—you couldn't change the volume or any other parameter—and immediately heard reflections off the surrounding environment. It was beautiful! When I beamed it at a wall I heard that the echoes that came back differed from the pulses that went out. If I aimed it at glass window I noticed that the echo was different from that which came from the wall. I visualized the sounds getting squashed on the impact. If we had perfect hearing, we should be able to tell how far away that wall is. Because sound travels about 1130 feet per second in air (under water it's five times faster), if it returns to you in a second, you can assume that the reflective surface is about 600 feet away. Half a second out, half a second back. The echoes are beautiful outdoors; you can hear the leaves on trees. By aiming the Sondol at certain angles one can create multiple echoes. They ricochet all over the room. Musicians ask to borrow my Sondols for concerts but I can't let them have them; they're one of a kind and can't be replaced if lost.

One night I had a vivid dream. (When you're deeply involved in a project, you start dreaming about it.) I saw humans—astronauts perhaps, I may have been one of them—exploring a dark space in an alien environment. They were beaming sound guns into darkened rooms, collecting information about those rooms and relaying it back to Earth. It was kind of a science fiction idea.

I bought four Sondols from *Listening Incorporated* and thought about making a performance piece. In those days you often didn't know how your piece was going to go until the day of the concert. In 1968 I was invited to Ann Arbor, Michigan, to the *Once Festival* Bob Ashley and Gordon Mumma had organized. I decided to present a piece with four performers playing Sondols. Not until the dress rehearsal was I clear about the form of the performance. Nothing in my training could help me organize the structure. I couldn't use what I'd learned in school because that had to do with notes and pitches and meters and rhythms. This piece had to do with pulse waves echoing off walls, ceilings, and floors of enclosed spaces.

The performance took place in the Michigan Union Ballroom, a huge space on the University of Michigan campus. I blindfolded the performers and stationed them in the four corners of the room. As a sort of prologue to the performance I walked around the room. My shoes, which had leather soles, made sharp, clicking sounds. I pulled apart the drapes on the windows to make the room more reverberant. I stacked up some chairs and positioned a couple of potted plants as obstacles. I hoped that the performers, as they approached the plants and chairs, would hear echoes coming back from them and could avoid walking into them.

Instead of writing a score that stipulates when each player plays and in what combinations I simply asked them to move to a central point in the darkened space, listening to their echoes as they moved. I gave them the task of orienting themselves in the dark, avoiding obstacles, and arriving at a predetermined goal. If they followed this simple task rather than imposing their own ideas about something musical everything would fall into place. For example, when four people are playing at the same time, the texture is so dense that none of them can hear his own echoes. The players have to stop playing every once in awhile to allow each other a clear sound-image to follow. So silence is built into the performance. I didn't indicate when it should occur. Stops, starts, silences, density, and texture are built into the task of orienting oneself by mean of echolocation. A performance of *Vespers* gives you an acoustic signature of the room, as if one were taking a slow sound photograph over a long period of time. You hear what the room sounds like. That was mysterious to me and wonderful. It really turned me on.

I called the piece *Vespers* for two reasons. Vespers is one of the seven canonical hours the Catholic Church held in the late afternoon or early evening. Although I am not religious I thought of it as a ritual in some way. *Vespers* also refers to the common bat of North America, of the family *vespertilionidae*. I wanted to pay homage to these courageous and supremely skillful creatures that are so maligned by our culture. Bats are just fabulous! They scoop up insects with their wings. They do all sorts of fancy things.

Once we performed *Vespers* in Finland. I had bought five hundred little toy crickets to take along with me. You know those metal toy crickets you can buy for a few cents each? They make sharp clicking sounds. Toward the end of the performance I passed a bunch of them out to people in the audience. Three hundred people or so began playing their crickets. The hall was ringing! The sound image of that room was marvelous. The room was being used as an instrument. Then a professor from the local music conservatory went out and got his violin. He started playing it in the middle of the performance. Can you believe that? People around him started making vulgar vocal sounds, or banal rhythms by clapping. If people were going to interfere with my pieces I wish they'd do something more interesting. I was depressed. After the concert as I was walking through the streets of Helsinki I could hear people that had been at the concert playing their little crickets. At two o'clock in the morning I could hear the loveliest trains of ticks and their accompanying echoes. It was beautiful. Some people finally got the point of the piece.

I Am Sitting in a Room

One day during the fall of 1968 I bumped into Edmond Dewan in the hallway of the Brandeis Music Department. In casual conversation he remarked that a professor at MIT named Bose had just given a lecture in which he described a way of testing a loudspeaker he was designing. He recycled sounds into his speakers to hear if their responses were flat. That's all I remember of our conversation. I picked up on the idea and decided to make some preliminary experiments in one of the practice rooms at Brandeis. I made sounds of various kinds and recycled them into the room over and over again. The results were strident; the room was too bright acoustically.

During the spring of 1969, I was living in an apartment at 454 High Street, Middletown, Connecticut. I was teaching during the spring semester at Wesleyan. It was a sordid habitat, the kind universities rent to part-time faculty. It had a green shag rug, heavy drapes on the windows, and an old armchair. I mention this because it has a lot to do with the acoustics of the room. The kitchen was supplied with one pot, a skillet, and a coffee cup. But that was okay; I was by myself and ate out a lot anyway.

One night I borrowed two Nagra tape recorders from the Music Department. They had purchased them for ethnological field recording. At that time Nagra machines were the *sine qua non* of the recording industry. They were the finest portable reel-to-reel recorders for films and field recording. Any Hollywood Western you ever saw was probably recorded with a Nagra. They were beautiful machines. I had a Beyer microphone, a single KLH loudspeaker, and a Dynaco amplifier. I set the mike up in the living room, sat down in the armchair, and wrote out a text that explained what I was about to do. In those days, there was a genre of work in which the process of the composition was the content of the work. I remember a Judson Church dancer, Trisha Brown I believe, describing her motions as she was doing them. I decided that the work would have no poetic or aesthetic content. The art was someplace else.

I placed the two machines on a table outside the door so the spinning reels wouldn't make noise. I unplugged the refrigerator, turned off the heat. I waited until the radiator pipes had cooled and the room got quiet. I waited until after 11 o'clock when a nearby bar, *The Three Coins*, closed. It was snowing that night so it was relatively quiet outside. There was not a lot of traffic going by. I went outside into the hallway, turned on one of the Nagras and, returning to the living room, read the text into the microphone. When I was finished, I went back out into the hallway, stopped the machine, rewound the tape, and listened to the results through headphones. The levels on the meters were okay. They hadn't peaked into the red zone. That would have indicated distortion. I transferred the tape to the second recorder, which was routed through the amplifier to the loudspeaker. I had positioned it on the chair I had been sitting in. I wanted the copy to sound as much like my original speech as possible. I wanted it to sound as if I were there in person actually talking in the room.

I went back outside the room and played this copy into the room again, recording it on the first recorder. I repeated this procedure until I had sixteen versions, one original and fifteen copies. I stayed up all night doing it. As the process continued more and more of the resonances of the room came forth; the intelligibility of the speech disappeared. Speech became music. It was magical.

I chose speech to test the space because it is rich in sounds. It has fundamental tones (formants) and lots of noisy stuff—p's, t's, s's, k's. It was crucial to avoid poetic references—poems, prayers, anything with high aesthetic value. I felt that would only get in the way. I wanted the acoustic exploration to be paramount, the room acoustics and it's gradual transformation to be the point of the piece.

Imagine a room so many meters long. Now imagine a sound wave that fits the room, which reflects off the wall in sync with itself. It will be louder (constructive interference). This is called a standing wave. If the wave doesn't fit it will bounce back out of sync and dissipate its energy (destructive interference). This is a simplistic model of what happens in *I Am Sitting in a Room*. All the components of my speech that related to the physical dimensions of the room are reinforced; those that don't, disappear. Think of yourself singing in the shower. You instinctively find the resonant frequency(-ies) of the small space you are in. Your voice sounds rich because it reinforces itself.

While the procedure of the work was repetitive, the rate of change of the resonance went at its own speed. I was careful not to influence the results in any way. I didn't raise or lower volume levels on purpose to make the process go faster or slower. I did have to carefully monitor the levels, however, in order to keep the recording from distorting or getting too soft. I did this minimally. I wanted the room to do the work.

I've made several versions of *I Am Sitting in a Room*, one for the dance *Dune* by Viola Farber, another in my house on 7 Miles Avenue. Each one sounds different. A couple of years ago some folks in Toulouse made several versions of the work. One of them was in a dialect peculiar to that region in France.

Chambers

In 1968, composer Pauline Oliveros, who was on the faculty of the University of California in San Diego, invited me out to be a guest artist. Every day I used to drive out on Route 1, along the ocean from La Jolla to Leucadia, and I would pass by a seashell shop. One day I stopped to buy several conch shells, some rather large. Pauline and I sawed the ends off them to make them into wind instruments. It's not the first time shells have been used as trumpets; they've been used in many cultures as that. I thought about when you're a child: you put a seashell up to your ear, and you hear the ocean. You hear the sounds around you resonating in the interior of the shell. I started to think of those shells as small rooms that had special resonant characteristics.

When I came home, I composed *Chambers*. The score consists of two lists: one is a collection of resonant objects one can find; the second is a list of ways of making them sound. It started as a conceptual piece that has several versions. One is that you find, collect, or make small resonant environments that you would put a sound in somehow, and hear the sound of the environment that the sound was originally made in in this new environment, and you would hear the change in the sound. I made a performance piece in 1968 for the Museum of Modern Art in New York. I gave everybody money and sent them out to buy materials for the performance. We had brought along suitcases, boots, bags, lunch boxes, vases, pots, pans, and other small, enclosed chambers. All we needed were sound sources that functioned by themselves. In a couple of hours the players came back with toy airplanes, trucks, sirens, whistles, radios, and electric shavers. Anything that was battery-operated or that you could wind up and would sound for a couple of minutes. Up until two hours before the concert we didn't know exactly what we were going to do. That's what you did in those days. You'd get an idea, go to the performance space, and execute it. You didn't rehearse or practice your part. I staged it simply. We started outside the room and came in through the doors. Each performer walked in with his sounding object. The performer simply walked through the room. The audience heard the movement of the sound, where it was going, and tried to figure out what was in it. I let each player decide where to put his chamber down. The performance consisted of bringing sounds into the space. You could hear the original or recorded sound in its chamber come through the space. That's all it was. The score for *Chambers* consists of lists of resonant spaces or objects—cisterns, bowls, bottles, etc.—along with ways of making them sound—rubbing, jiggling, burning, etc.

In 1994 we had a festival here of my work. I wanted Wesleyan students to participate in it, so I asked the students in Music 109 to collect resonant objects and sounds. We performed it at noontime in Crowell Hall. Everybody carried in their object, one by one, and filled up the hall with sounds. There were about sixty performers finally sitting on stage with their objects. It was wonderful. The sounds were so quiet and the texture so thick.

I've also done *Chambers* as an installation. I collected sixteen objects when I was performing in Europe. I bought some pots and pans in Amsterdam, and various things, and then I recorded environmental sounds with a cassette tape recorder. I would get on a tram, for example, and record a sound for an hour or so. I made a lot of recordings of public spaces. In large restaurants, you can hear the sounds of forks and knives, of tinkling glasses. You can get a sonic idea of the activities in those spaces. For installations I simply mount the resonant objects on sculpture stands. My favorite one was the sound of the huge railroad station in Cologne, Germany, heard inside a thimble. I used a single earphone as a loudspeaker. Visitors walk in and hear all these sounds in funny little objects.

A few weeks ago two players did a version of *Chambers* at the Greenwich House Music School in New York. They played garden hoses as wind instruments, starting outside the small concert hall. One slowly climbed a stairway up several flights playing as he went; the other walked downstairs and outside into a courtyard a couple of floors below. The dispersal of the sounds as they receded into the distance was beautiful.

9
BELL LABS

Blue Suede

I first came across James Tenney in New York in the Sixties. He and Malcolm Goldstein and Philip Corner had organized *The Tone Roads Ensemble* (*Tone Roads* is the title of a set of pieces by Charles Ives), which gave concerts of new music. It was wonderful to go to New York and hear the music of John Cage, Edgard Varèse, Henry Cowell, and Morton Feldman. It was the first time we heard this music. Jim played the piano and conducted the ensemble.

Jim had made several electronic pieces when he was still in college. One was called *Blue Suede* (1961), a tape collage of the Elvis Presley song. That was a wild number in those days. The line, "You can do anything, but lay off of my blue suede shoes," was shocking. Can you imagine that? You know what a collage is, don't you? Around 1912 or so the Cubist painters Picasso and Braque started affixing foreign objects to their canvases. They took things from everyday life, fragments of newspapers, objects, any found visual material, and overlaid or juxtaposed them on a canvas or other flat surface. It was a wonderful technique for putting unlikely images next to each other, bypassing the painting process and using materials that hitherto you would re-create or imitate. It took the art out of the art, in a strange way. Perhaps the advent of the photograph had something to do with it; you didn't need to render reality anymore by painting it. Children in kindergarten make collages nowadays; they can be creative without having to draw or paint the actual images. *Blue Suede* is more a rearrangement of materials from a single source than a collage of bits and pieces from different sources. All the juxtapositions were spliced on tape with a razor blade.

Noise Study

In the early Sixties Jim worked as a resident artist at Bell Labs, in New Jersey, making electronic pieces on tape and using their computers. At that time he was using Max Matthews' Music IV, one of the first computer languages for popular use. The composer would design his or her own instruments. The word "instrument" is used here in a broad sense. A sine wave, for example, can be depicted on an oscilloscope as a sine curve. In a computer, if you can describe enough points along that curve, you can design your own sine wave oscillator. It doesn't exist in the physical world; it's imaginary. All you need is a fast enough sampling rate to make the wave smooth. You can also make any imaginable waveform. The astonishing thing was that you're not dealing with electronic components. You weren't pinned down to physical devices—audio oscillators, filters, and the like. You could design any device in the digital computer that previously existed in the analog studio.

Jim came out of his two and a half years at Bell Labs with a set of six pieces on tape. One of them was *Analog No. 1: Noise Study*. Why would he call a work made by digital synthesis analog? Perhaps the reason is that even though the sounds are made digitally they are recorded on analog tape and superimposed—up to fifteen tracks—to get the density Jim wanted, which would have taken up too much memory in the computer. The sound source for the entire piece was white noise. Jim imitated traffic sounds by sweeping white noise up and down with a filter. He says he got the idea for the piece while driving to New Jersey from Manhattan every day through the Holland Tunnel. At first the traffic sounds bothered him. Then he started paying attention to the sounds in the tunnel and began to find them fascinating. Recently, I drove through the Holland Tunnel on my way to Pennsylvania. I heard two layers of sound: one was a mid-range to high swishing sound, probably made by the automobile tires; the other was a lower continuous sound, made by the motors. Both strands of sound were continuous and undulating. I got the image of an enormous flute being played by the fans that blow the bad air out of the Tunnel. It was fascinating, listening to these sounds. I probably wouldn't have been so aware of them without having heard Jim's *Noise Study*.

For Ann (Rising)

The title, *For Ann (Rising)* (1969), is a lovely pun on the name of Jim's first wife, Ann Reising. The piece consists of overlapping sine tones that start below human audibility and sweep up out of our range of hearing. There are twelve ascending waves; each one starts a minor sixth interval below the preceding one.

People get this phenomenon confused with Shepard tones, named after Roger Shepard, who was a Bell Lab scientist at the same time Jim worked there in the Sixties. He developed a phenomenon in which ascending chromatic tones sound as if they never get to where they are going. Each tone is constructed by the superposition of sine waves separated by octaves. Imagine a loud tone doubled by a soft tone an octave below it. As the scale ascends the upper (loud) tones become softer while the lower (soft) tones become louder. At the midpoint both tones are of equal loudness. As the upper tone fades out the bottom one—now the upper—is at its loudest. And so forth up the scale. You have the illusion of going nowhere. It never ends. It's similar to M. C. Escher's 1960 lithograph *Ascending and Descending*. You climb up the stairs over and over again but never reach the top. French composer Jean-Claude Risset created a version of the Shepard Scale in which the steps between each tone are continuous. It's called the *Shepard-Risset Glissando.* It's this sliding version that resembles Tenney's composition.

For Ann (Rising) is one of the classic pieces of minimalism; it challenges your idea of what a piece of music might be. Some people might say it's more like a scientific exploration. It's so clear, it's based on such a simple idea. The form is inexorable. You know it's not going to change once it starts. This version lasts about eleven minutes. It's a beautiful example of a single-minded form. Once it begins you know it won't change. But as you listen your focus constantly changes, that is, your attention switches back and forth from one ascending gliss to another as they fade in and out from below to above audibility. Your mind is extremely active; you become an active participant in the performance. It is perhaps this attribute that distinguishes experimental music from more conventional avant-garde music: the form doesn't lead you around but invites you to participate more closely and personally.

Having Never Written a Note for Percussion

Every once in a while in the Seventies, I'd go to my mailbox and there'd be a postcard from Jim Tenney. On it would be a score of one of his pieces. He called them his *Postal Pieces.* He made about ten in all. Each one was dedicated to a friend. Let's look at one of them.

Having Never Written a Note for Percussion was written in 1971. The score consists simply of a roll, a couple of hairpins (crescendo and diminuendo markings), some dynamic markings, and a fermata. The structure is very simple. The player simply rolls continuously while making a long gradual crescendo from quadruple pianissimo (as soft as you can play) to a quadruple fortissimo climax (as loud as you can play) and back again. The crescendo and diminuendo are completely smooth and linear, but the musical results are not; the gong steps into different modes of vibration. It's as if it warms up, reaches a threshold of resonance, then, even though the player is rolling gradually, it steps abruptly into a louder mode. The points at which that happens form the structure of the work. By sweeping the dynamic range from extremely soft to extremely loud, you discover the locations of the modes of vibration. The piece has two structures then: a gradual one, and sudden ones. You don't know beforehand where the resonant peaks are going to occur. Even more astonishing is that when the player is sustaining a high level of loudness, the sound builds up and then drops suddenly and starts building up again. The score says that it may be played on any percussion instrument. It could be played on a snare drum, bass drum, or a kettledrum, for example. The gong, however, is a great acoustic instrument. It's so complicated in the way it vibrates. There are gongs in China that, struck at night, can still be heard sounding at dawn.

10

LENSES, INTERVALS

Handphone Table

Laurie Anderson is best known as a multimedia performance and recording artist. She makes large-scale performance works and even wrote an immensely popular song, "O Superman," which got to second place on the pop charts in England in 1981. I include her in this book because early in her career she invented several fascinating instruments. In 1977, with the help of Bob Bielecki, she invented the Tape-Bow Violin consisting of a strand of pre-recorded audiotape on the bow instead of horsehair. A magnetic tape head is placed on the bridge of the violin. When she bows the violin the pre-recorded sounds are heard. The speed at which she bows controls the pitch of the sounds on the tape. If she bows slowly, the sounds are low and slow; the faster she bows the higher and faster the sounds. Bielecki designed and built a quiver of bows each with different sound material.

In 1978 she created the *Handphone Table*. You would sit at a table with your elbows on it, hands resting on your cheekbones. Low sounds would come to you from a speaker under the table by means of bone conduction. Low sounds were necessary because they travel more easily than higher sounds through one's bone structure. It was a wonderful idea. In that same year she designed an acoustic lens at the Franklin Institute in Philadelphia. Bielecki constructed a sphere made out of a thin latex material. It was inflated with CO_2 and inserted in a wall between two rooms. Sounds from one room were played through the sphere that focused them to a spot in the other room. Bob once confided to me that it didn't work too well but the idea was there.

Heavier Than Air

In 1988 I made a performance piece on the same principle called *Heavier Than Air*. Several performers whispered sentences from Joe Brainard's book *I Remember* through CO_2-inflated balloons held in front of their mouths while slowly changing the direction of the balloons from left to right and back, focusing the sounds to listeners in various parts of the room. I used whispering because the high frequencies of whispers have short wavelengths that travel through the balloons easily. The long wavelengths of lower frequencies would have flowed around the balloons, not through them. Sound waves are not particularly directional; they want to spread out from their source. As the waves flow through the balloons they travel more slowly in the middle than at the edges because the balloon is round. It's thicker in the middle. It takes longer for the waves to pass through, flattening them, and causing the waves to exit on a flat plane on the other side, focusing them in a narrow beam.

Composition 1960 #7

When I taught ear training years ago, I played intervals on the piano for the students to identify. All I had to do was to play an interval once or twice and most students could identify it. Even if the piano were out of tune, the gross approximation was enough. Music is filled with intervals. Stacked on top of each other they make chords; stretched out horizontally they form melodies. They don't exist for their own sake, but as the building blocks of melody and harmony. But what if you're interested in the nature of the interval itself? When I was a student at Yale we read Paul Hindemith's theory books. Paul Hindemith was a famous German composer whose music and theories dominated American music, at least as it existed in colleges and universities, for many years. He established a hierarchy of musical intervals based on the overtone series, going from consonance to dissonance. We spent a good deal of time listening to intervals, trying to get a sense of their weights and feelings. What if you wanted to put an interval under an aural microscope and discover what's really there? How would you closely examine something as impalpable as a musical interval? One way is to play it loudly; another, repeat it many times; third, sustain it for a long time.

In 1960 La Monte Young composed fifteen short prose pieces. Some are fanciful, offering the reader an image or idea to ponder. Others are simple instructions for actions to be made. In *Composition 1960 #7* the intervals of a perfect fifth is simply "to be held a long time."

The interval of a perfect fifth appears in the overtone series as the second and third partials above a fundamental tone. Starting on B, the second and third overtone will be B, an octave above the fundamental, and F-sharp, a fifth above that. Any two tones with a ratio of 3:2 will give you a perfect fifth. But what if one of the pitches is a little flat or sharp, what is the ratio then? How long would it take the interval to sound exactly the same way? You can see that in order to fully perceive an interval, you have to stay with it a long time. There's no device in the world that can give you a perfect 3:2 ratio, no oscillators that can be tuned that precisely. There aren't any singers who can do that either. The reason La Monte Young is interested in long durations is to accurately measure intervals that change slightly over time.

The frequency of alternating current in the United States is 60 cycles per second. That's close to B-natural two octaves below middle C, which is tuned to around 62 cps. Perhaps La Monte chose B-natural to tune to our electronic environment. If you stay with it for a long enough time you begin to hear the overtones that are generated above the two pitches. You hear the overtone series on B-natural and F-sharp. You can see that these overtones match in several places, particularly if you tune the fifth in a perfect ratio of 3:2. But if one of the tones slips a little bit, the interval no longer has a simple ratio but rather something extraordinarily complex. Then the overtones don't line up exactly. For Young a perfect fifth is an acoustical tester that can generate overtones, the clashes of which are endlessly interesting, if you pay attention to them. If you spent several days with a perfect fifth, you'd hear the most unusual things. La Monte removes the imagery of music to get at the presence of sound. If there's anything in this piece, it's the presence of those intervals in the room. You don't remember the past or anticipate the future, you're in the present. There's no such thing as a perfect fifth, except in an idealized sense. You can only approach it by spending a long time with it; the longer you spend, the better resolution you get.

B-natural and F-sharp are within the voice range of very person in this room. B may be a little high for men unaccustomed to singing, but with a little help any male can do it. F-sharp is comfortable for any soprano. Altos and tenors can sing either pitch. It's a unisex piece. Let's pack up our book bags and go into the tunnel under the Music Studios, the acoustics there are very reverberant. I brought along a pitch pipe. (Your professor is prepared.) Did you see the movie *Quest for Fire*? It was about a prehistoric clan of humans who carried fire along with them wherever they went. Let's carry our perfect fifth with us into the tunnels and perform La Monte Young's *Composition 1960 #7*.

11

TAPE RECORDERS

Come Out

It's shocking to realize how old-fashioned reel-to-reel tape recorders have become. When I started, they were the work-horses for composing electronic music. Now everything is digital, and there is little need for tape recorders any more; everything can be stored in the memory of a computer. Tape recorders were discovered during World War II. The Allies were monitoring broadcasts in Germany and every once in a while they would hear a radio concert at 2 o'clock A.M. It was hardly likely that an orchestra would be playing at that late hour in Stuttgart. It sounded so clear. It was only after the war they discovered large boxes containing the first tape recorders in one of the German radio stations. Before that there were wire recorders, which sounded awful, or you could record directly onto disk. Of course, if you made a mistake, there was no way to edit it out. With tape, however, you could remove mistakes with a razor blade. Tape was quiet, too, and you could record a lot of material on a single reel. It became the new technology. Most of the pieces of early tape music used the machines to play back the completed compositions. The three pieces I'm going to talk about now are ones in which the tape recorder itself is used more directly in the compositional process.

Come Out (1966) by Steve Reich was composed for a benefit for six young men arrested for murder during the Harlem riots of 1964. One young man, who was subsequently acquitted, described being beaten by police. He explained that if you were bleeding visibly, you would be taken to the hospital instead of being kept in jail. So he squeezed a bruise on his leg, forcing blood to emerge. He said, "I had to, like, open the bruise up and let some of the bruise blood come out to show them." Steve used a recording of this sentence as source material for the work.

First Steve copied the sentence on tape three times; then he extracted the last five words, "come out to show them," and made a tape loop out of them, which he copied repeatedly onto two reels of tape. Don't be confused by the term "loop." It may mean a length of tape joined together at both ends or a sample of music repeated over and over again. He synchronized the tapes and played them on two tape recorders. After letting them play awhile they gradually started to move apart. No two machines go at exactly the same speed, even the best ones you can find. One speeds up, and whatever material is on the tape moves ahead of the other. The loops move out of phase. You begin to hear the phrase slightly ahead of its twin. The two identical sounds slightly out of sync created a third sound. By letting the recorders move at their own speed, and not treating the variation in speed as a defect, Reich discovered phase in music. It was a great discovery. It was as if a miracle were happening.

I first heard *Come Out* in Antioch, Ohio. The Sonic Arts Union was performing there and David Behrman, who had just produced a series of new music recordings for Columbia Records, played it for us. What a shock it was! We had never heard anything like it before. What was amazing was that you could hear a piece of music composing itself. Before this you would make material and then present it already made, or you would use part of it, or you would take the end result as a sound image. Once the process in *Come Out* starts, the composer doesn't step in except to split and multiply the images in some way at two junctures in the recording. The composer doesn't decide what's happening from moment to moment. The first time that I heard it, it was like a light bulb going on over my head. It was something really wonderful and new. It was new in the way it directly used the technology and also in the way Steve thought about what a musical form can be.

Night Music

The characteristic of magnetic recording tape is non-linear. If it were used as is, an output of high distortion would result. To correct this, a bias current is applied to the record head to magnetize the tape on the correct position of its characteristic curve. The frequency of the bias current is high—from 60 to 100 kilocycles—so that it doesn't interfere with the material being recorded.

In *Night Music* (1960), Richard Maxfield used the bias frequency of a tape recorder as a found oscillator. He used the sawtooth wave output from an oscilloscope to beat against it. The sound sources are too high to hear, but you can hear the resultant tones. It was a magical idea.

Resultant tones, also known as difference or combination tones, occur in various manifestations in the world of electronics, acoustics, and music. Under certain conditions, when two signals or musical tones are sounded, the difference between them may result. For example, if musical tones of, say, 400 and 500 cycles per second are sounded, a difference tone of 100 cps may be heard. FM and AM radio works on this principle. In FM (frequency modulation), a carrier frequency is modulated by extremely rapid changes in frequency. In AM the carrier frequency is modulated by rapid changes in loudness. Amazing phenomena!

The title *Night Music* invokes the sounds of birds, insects, tree toads, and other natural sounds you might hear during a summer night. The sounds, recorded entirely on tape, sound uncannily natural. They are all made electronically, however; birds and insects make their sounds mechanically. Crickets scrape the serrated edges of their wings, vibrating a resonant region called the harp. Cicadas tense and relax muscles surrounding a thin membrane similar to a drumhead. When the muscles are released they cause the membrane to snap, making a clicking sound. They can do this up to 480 times a second. Some drummers! They have even developed an air sac around the membrane that is tuned to its resonant frequency, making the clicks louder (mechanical amplifier). Each cicada has its own song, too. The cicada is not the only creature to use a natural resonator to amplify its sounds. Bornean tree-hole frogs (*Metaphrynella sundana*), for example, tune their songs to the resonant frequencies of partially water-filled hollows in trees. As the water rises and falls in the hole, the frogs alter the pitch of their songs. Some musicians!

Many birds make simple vocalizations analogous to a sweeping sine wave oscillator. Their songs simply consist of upward and downward slurs. Others use frequency and amplitude modulation to make more complex warbles and twitters. Some have two sets of oscillator systems that operate independently or simultaneously. It's remarkable that creatures from the natural world utilize concepts that we use in our technological world. It makes you wonder what is natural and what is not.

I of IV

I of IV (1966) by Pauline Oliveros was composed in real time, no editing, no splicing. The materials consist of two stereo tape recorders, a couple of mixers, twelve audio oscillators, and reverb. Guess why there would be twelve oscillators in this studio? Answer: the twelve notes of the scale. In making *I of IV* Pauline used two kinds of delaying techniques: head delay and tape delay. On any professional tape recorder the audio tape passes over three heads: the erase head which erases any pre-recorded material that might be on the tape; a record head which records the sounds of the input signal; and a playback head which plays back the recorded sounds. Most good machines have an A/B switch, which enables you to hear what is being recorded and what is being played back. Since the heads are physically spaced apart, you can get short time lags between what goes in to the machine and what comes out. The distance between the record and playback heads varies from machine to machine. A distance of two inches gives a 266 millisecond (a quarter of a second) delay, if the tape is running at 7.5 inches per second, 133 ms at 15 ips. Pauline calls that reiterative delay. Did any of you see the movie *Patton*? As George C. Scott (Patton) is looking over an ancient battlefield in Sicily, you hear a trumpet call overlapping itself several times at short intervals. It was probably made with head delay. You've heard that effect every once in awhile in movies and on television. You can in addition feed the playback signal back into the record head, causing reverberation. Pauline got longer, eight second delays by threading the tape from the supply reel on the first recorder to the take-up reel on the second, positioned five feet away: eight seconds at 7.5 ips equals sixty inches.

You can feed anything you want back into anything you want. You could take the record head signal, take the playback signal, bring it back into the record head. There's no reason you can't make feedback loops within the machine itself, by feeding the playback output back into the record input and so forth. For sound sources she used eleven sine waves (pure waves, no overtones), and one square wave (rough sounding, every odd overtone). The sine waves were tuned above audibility (20,000 cps), the square wave, below one cycle. Combination tones were created among the high frequency oscillators, plus the bias frequency of the recorder. All were pulse-modulated by the sub-audio signal. They all go through reverb, which gives them spaciousness, some through reiterative short delays, others through longer tape delays.

Tape delay was a wonderful tool to make electronic music in live performance. The trick is to design the configuration in such a way that the delays are not heard as periodic. You have to be able to forget them. Let's play a little of *I of IV*. It sounds like a living organism. Let's listen for things to come back. Oh, I love that one!

When is it going to come back? There it is! You can measure the length of the delay by listening for when the sounds return. It's wonderful to talk about these old-fashioned compositional techniques. It's like talking about the *viola da gamba*.

12

REPETITION

In C

"In C" is a phrase used by jazz musicians to indicate improvising in the key of C. When you go to an engagement and want to warm up, the leader might simply say to the other players, "In C," and they know what he means. Jamming (improvising) is a good way to get to know new players. *In C* (1964) by Terry Riley, is for any number of players of treble instruments, that is, instruments in the range from middle C and above. The score consists of fifty-three melodic cells, many of which you might find in a Baroque or Classical work. Each one has a double bar before and after it, indicating that it can be repeated as many times as the player wishes. Each player must play all fifty-three cells in order. You can't go back to a previous one. Throughout the performance a pianist plays the top two Cs of the piano as a rapid eighth-note pulse, which sets the tempo of the performance. The pulse remains constant; it doesn't slow down or speed up. Each player synchronizes his playing with the pulse. There are all sorts of internal decisions you have to make about moving forward. You have to have a sense of ensemble. Terry was an accomplished improviser so this was a natural thing for him to do. A typical performance takes about forty-five minutes.

You probably know that the key of C major has no accidentals, no flats or sharps. If you started on the note C on the piano and stuck to the white keys, you would most likely be playing in the key of C. If you introduce a black note, a flat or a sharp, you will most likely be playing in another key. Adding a sharp or flat to the key signature brings you to a key a fifth above or below the previous key. G major, one sharp, is a fifth above C; F major, with one flat, is a fifth below. The closest key relationships are those one or two accidentals apart. In Western classical music, composers would usually move (modulate) to a closely related key. Later in the nineteenth century, for reasons of drama, modulations to more distant keys became more common. You can get a good picture of these relationships by drawing a circle of fifths: moving clockwise, adding sharps, you arrive at the key of B-sharp major, which is actually C major; moving counterclockwise, adding flats, you arrive at D-double flat, actually C major.

Let's look at Terry's cells in chronological order. The first cell actually starts on the note E, preceded by a grace note C. Starting on E, the third degree of the C major scale, gives the beginning of the work a feeling of lightness. You're not hammering away at the tonic. The piece may be in C but you can't be sure yet. It's only at cell number six that C appears as a long tone. The first accidental we encounter, at cell number fourteen, is an F-sharp leading up to G. This gives a feeling of movement towards G-major. But since some of the other players may still be playing the previous two or three cells, depending upon how far apart they are, the movement is somewhat blurred. Let's superimpose the two previous cells being played by slower players. We find a cluster of the following pitches: F-natural, F-sharp, G, B, and C. It creates a lovely mixture of the tonic (C) with the dominant (G) and the sub-dominant (F). B and F-sharp are both leading tones (to C and G), further reinforcing their presence. This cluster is almost Stravinskyan in its polytonal sound. The piece ends when everyone has played the last cell. They may stop at any time. The pulse simply stops any time after that.

The addition of the pulse was most likely Steve Reich's idea. There is controversy about this. He played in the first performance of *In C*. To position the pulse in the highest octave of the piano was a stroke of genius. It would have been more conventional to place it in a lower bass octave. It would have more power because of its heaviness, but the harmonics would have tended to obscure the higher instrumental sounds that are supposed to be above middle C. Instead, the forty-five-minute performance maintains the original lightness and clarity. A smart idea!

1 + 1

Philip Glass's *1 + 1* (1967) is a prototype in miniature of the essential idea that permeates all of his early music. It consists of only two rhythmic cells: an eighth note and two sixteenth notes followed by an eighth.

First, a mini-lesson in rhythmic notation. Let's start with a quarter note, which is indicated by a black oval with a stem on it. Two quarter notes equal a half note, indicated by an open oval with a stem; four quarter notes equal a whole note, open oval, no stem. Let's divide the quarter note: two eighths, black ovals with stems and flags, equal one quarter. Two sixteenths, two flags, equal one eighth. When two or more eighths or sixteenths are played together they may be connected by beams. A sixteenth subdivides into two thirty-second notes. Of course durations are relative, depending on the tempo. You could make a whole note as short as an eighth note by indicating a fast enough tempo. Starting with a quarter note at sixty beats a minute, a whole note at two hundred and forty would match an eighth note at thirty. But seeing whole notes strongly suggests long durations, eighths shorter ones. Philip simply suggests a fast tempo for *1 + 1*. The player has to decide what fast is. A 120 beat per minute cadence is normal for a marching band on Memorial Day. College football bands march much faster, to show how much pep they have.

Tempos can be accurately indicated by metronome markings. A metronome is a device that produces a steady beat or flashing light to establish beats per minute for practice purposes or for composers to set the tempo of their compositions. The metronome was invented by a Dutchman named Winkel in 1812, but Johann Mälzel copied the idea and is credited with the invention.

Beethoven was the first well-known composer to use metronome markings in his music. In many modern scores you will find "MM = (some number of beats)."

Philip devised a simple process whereby anyone can build a flowing musical continuity. You simply string the two elements together making rhythmic phrases by adding beats. For example: ba-ba boom, ba-ba-boom, boom, ba-ba-boom, boom, boom, ba-ba-boom, boom, boom, boom, ba-ba-boom, boom, boom, ba-ba-boom, boom, ba-ba-boom. I started with two sixteenths and an eighth; then I added an eighth to get two sixteenths and two eighths, then three, and four until I got two sixteenths and four eighths. Then, subtracting one eighth at a time I got back to the original two sixteenths and one eighth.

There are no rules really except you don't use any other rhythmic figures, such as a triplets or quadruplets. You simply generate a form by adding and subtracting the two elements. Let's write one. This is a wonderful exercise. It enables you to compose a little piece you can actually play. Experienced drummers can actually improvise this work.

The instructions are to play with the knuckles or fingertips on an amplified tabletop. Several years ago I asked an undergraduate percussionist to perform *1 + 1*. The day before the concert he had a bicycle accident. He broke his knuckles. He showed up to the rehearsal, smiling, with huge white bandages on his hands. Even though he was unable to perform, we all had a good laugh about it.

I performed *1 + 1* a few years ago when Philip was here as an homage to him. I was so afraid I'd get lost in the middle of the performance I wrote most of the rhythmic figures out on paper. I performed it too expressively, too. I made it too musical, relying on crescendos and diminuendos to get me through. I was afraid to let the rhythms be themselves. You get beautiful asymmetric structures. Even though the pulse is steady the number of times the cells are repeated changes. You get unexpected results.

That's the way Philip thought in his early days. He got the idea of adding and subtracting notes to build flowing musical structures partly from the study of Indian music. He was trained in Western classical contemporary music that was complex, atonal and often rhythmically unplayable. While he was studying with Nadia Boulanger, in Paris, he met Indian musician Ravi Shankar. Shankar had been hired to compose a film score and he didn't know Western notation. There was no reason he would, Indian music isn't notated in that way. So he hired Philip to help him. That was Phil's introduction to Indian music. There's no harmony, no chords in Indian music. There's no bass line that carries the music forward. What you have are very intricate and complex melodic and rhythmic structures. They're actually more complex than in Western music. The emphasis is on rhythm and melody. The opening of the Beethoven Seventh Symphony, for example, consists of just two chords. Nothing could be simpler than that. The rhythm makes it unforgettably beautiful.

Music in Fifths

Music in Fifths is made out of parallel fifths. I don't know any music that moves so continuously in parallel motion except some parts of the music of Debussy and jazz. But in *Music In Fifths* Philip is stressing horizontal movement, he doesn't need harmony.

We've encountered the perfect fifth before, haven't we? In harmony, where you want the flow of the chords to be natural and strong in themselves, you don't want anything to stick out. Fifths are acoustically so strong that when they move in parallel they call attention to themselves. When I was a student, you'd get marked down for writing a parallel fifth in a harmony exercise.

Looking through the chorales of Bach, you (almost) never find a parallel fifth. The first thing that Mlle. Boulanger would get her American students to do was work on harmony. Before they wrote any pieces she'd get them to do harmonic exercises at the keyboard so they could fluently play melodies and harmonize them. She was very strict about the rules. And one of the rules was not to write any parallel fifths. Once she had a student named Jean Françaix who was always writing parallel fifths. The story goes that whenever he wrote one she would send him down the stairs to run around the block. It's probably not a true story but it illustrates the importance, at least for Boulanger, of avoiding parallel fifths. Anyway, Philip Glass went to Paris to study with Mlle. Boulanger. One of the first pieces he wrote when he got home was *Music in Fifths*. Written in 1969, it begins with a simple diatonic eight-note five-finger exercise. When you study piano as a beginner, you practice exercises that fit comfortably under your fingers. You don't have to change your hand position. The next figure repeats the first pair of notes making a ten-note figure. The next repeats the last two notes so now you have a twelve-note figure. Glass keeps repeating various groups of notes until he has made a twenty-six-note phrase. By the end of the sequence the original eight-note figure has grown without the addition of any new pitches. He hasn't added any new notes. He's just repeated notes that are all ready there.

How do we listen to this music? Do you find that you're counting while you're listening? Are you waiting to see whether the next phrase is going to be longer or shorter? It's different from other music. One listener told me he sees a graph being plotted. Another said he keeps wanting to be able to read the phrase as starting at a different point, but that never quite happens. He always feels the overall meter of that segment, even though it changes. He was expecting it to change enough that he'd begin to lose track of the beginning and end. He said he doesn't lose track of the beginning, it might be more interesting if he did. It means always finding a tonic. No matter where you go, you always hear the C as the tonic. And some pieces that repeat and shift patterns all the time, you're reinventing what and where the tonic is. You're always in a state of shift. Philip does rhythmically what you were describing, you don't identify a downbeat. Is that what you're saying? You do hear the downbeat? It's this feeling you have as it's moving up the scale and back down. The length of the phrase changes. Yes, that's because the lower note is the tonic and no matter what he does you always hear that as a downbeat. Does everybody hear it that way?

Music in Similar Motion

Let's talk a little bit about the various types of motion you can have between two voices. The word *voice* can mean a musical instrument as well as a human voice. In writing simple four-part harmony, there are four ways of moving a pair of voices. If they move in opposite directions that's called contrary motion. If they move in the same direction, keeping the same distance between them, that's parallel motion. If they move in the same direction but vary the distance between them, that's similar motion. And if one voice stays still while the other moves in either direction, up or down, that's called oblique motion. So in *Music in Similar Motion* everybody moves in the same direction but doesn't necessarily keep the same distance apart.

Music in Twelve Parts

Music in Twelve Parts (1971–1974), a large-scale work from the early Seventies, was an encyclopedia of Phil's musical ideas at that time. These included the additive and subtractive processes, diminution, augmentation, as well as shifting musical materials in cyclical patterns. For example, one voice might be in three, another in four, causing overlappings. One is going one, two, three and the other is going one, two, three, four. It takes twelve repetitions before they come back in sync. Augmentation means taking a melody and stretching it out into longer durations. That's a way to make a piece grow. The opposite of augmentation is diminution, shortening the note values so that the music proceeds more quickly, in double or triple time, for example. It seems as if Philip was going back and investigating earlier forms of music.

The story goes that Phil composed one piece that he called *Music in Twelve Parts* because it consisted of twelve separate lines or parts. One day a friend asked him where the other eleven pieces were. So Phil simply wrote eleven more parts. Tim Page says that there is a hidden drone in all twelve pieces, that is, the presence of C-sharp and F-sharp is heard in every measure. There is also some humor in the last piece. Phil introduces a twelve-tone row at the end as if whisking that style of writing out of his life forever. But to my ears it sounds wonderful and I wish that he had explored atonality a bit more in his later pieces even if only to avoid some of the sameness his music has.

Clapping Music

Steve Reich got the idea for *Clapping Music* in a Spanish restaurant in Brussels. In the late Sixties and early Seventies when we went to Brussels to perform we'd end up there after the concert. The food was cheap and the wine was passable. Steve was watching a troupe of Spanish flamenco dancers clapping their hands in interlocking patterns. He was fascinated by it. Interlocking is a structural device common to musics of many cultures, including Indonesia and West Africa. In medieval Western art music the hocket ("hiccup") is made by two players sharing a common rhythmic and melodic motive. It was done for the sake of breathing or to split up the rhythmic and melodic patterns among a group of players.

Clapping Music is composed solely on a single twelve-beat

rhythmic pattern. The score has no staff lines because there are no pitches. Both clappers repeat the twelve-beat pattern twelve times simultaneously. After twelve repetitions, the first player steps ahead an eighth-note, continuing to play the same pattern. The first clapper repeats the same pattern throughout the piece. After twelve repetitions, the second clapper steps ahead again. He's now a quarter note ahead. Every twelve measures the second clapper steps ahead one eighth note. After twelve repetitions he's back in unison with the first clapper. It's that simple.

What's uncanny about *Clapping Music* is that each composite pattern has a totally different feel to it. Let's take a look at a couple of different ones.

Violin Phase

Violin Phase is a formal extension and expansion of *Clapping Music*. It has a beautiful structure. It's written for four violins, but is often performed with one live player and three recorded tape tracks. It's too difficult to play with four violins. All the material is contained in a twelve-note phrase in the key of A major. Twelve is a wonderful musical number. There are twelve notes in a chromatic scale and, rhythmically, you can divide twelve into groups of three and four—an uneven and an even number. It's a powerful structural tool. Many African drum patterns are in twelve. Steve Reich, in fact, visited Wesleyan a number of times in the Seventies to play with Abraham Adzenyah, our West African drummer, and experienced these patterns first hand.

Let's look at the twelve-beat phrase. Since it contains all the material for a large-scale work one might expect it to be as varied as possible. Quite the opposite is true. It's static. It consists of a six-beat upward gesture followed by its exact repetition, except that the last beat of the first gesture is tied over one beat extending it to seven beats and shortening the second one to five beats. Two identical gestures separated by a small glitch. The glitch is more than a one-time syncopation, because as the work progresses the twelve-beat phrase gets delayed against itself and the glitch keeps gradually appearing, becoming an important rhythmic event. Each gesture contains two double stops, that is, two tones played at the same time. Double stops are sustainable provided the tones are on adjacent strings. Triple and quadruple stops are not sustainable. The bow cannot smoothly glide over three or four strings because they are positioned in a curve over the bridge. They may be played as arpeggios, however.

In the larger structure what happens is this: the violinist records the phrase as a loop on one track of a four-track machine. The same loop is re-recorded on a second track, starting four beats ahead of the first loop. The same procedure is repeated on a third track, eight beats ahead. One track remains empty because it's being played by the solo violin. In a performance a violinist stands between two loudspeakers. The volume control for one of the tracks is raised. The other tracks are running along silently. The soloist plays in sync with the one sounding track. In a recording studio he uses headphones, so he's in sync before the track is brought up. The phrase repeats several times. After awhile the violinist starts gradually accelerating, moving ahead of the recorded loop until he is one eighth note ahead. Now you have a canon or round at an eighth note delay. *Row, Row, Row Your Boat* is a simple canon. The canon is a useful musical form because it enables a composer to spin out music in long strands from one set of materials. You simply write a melody, then copy it in another voice, and write something underneath or above it, adding that to the original melody. What's different about this is that the player gradually moves ahead of an exact copy of itself. You actually hear the canon being made in real time. In Western classical music there has long been the practice of speeding up (accelerando) to generate excitement or establish a new tempo and slowing down (decelerando) to signal the end of a piece. But in this work the performer is asked to move gradually over time to make new relationships. That's a new idea.

The player continues to move gradually ahead until he or she is four eighth notes ahead of the original twelve-note phrase. This puts the player in sync with one of the tracks that has been playing along silently. Now the engineer raises the volume of that track. You now hear a canon consisting of two copies of the twelve-note phrase, one on top of the other, four beats apart. At this point, the violinist begins to extract melodic and rhythmic material from the composite sounds of those two tracks. He or she pulls out of the texture new rhythmic and melodic cells. He can't invent new material or slow down or speed up. He doesn't improvise freely, but creates new patterns from the composite material. The player decides on that before the performance. Steve leaves nothing to chance. He doesn't believe in inspiration at the moment. He thinks that preparation, concentration, and focus give you a more valuable result. Quite the opposite from Cage. As soon as the player feels he has exhausted the material he or she gradually moves ahead four beats to where the third track is. As that track's volume level is raised the player now invents melodic and rhythmic structures from the composite material of the three simultaneously sounding tracks. The tracks enter one after the other. Once they're in, they stay in. There's more happening at the end of the piece. It's a very clear form.

In classical Western music variations occur in chronological order. The theme is stated first, then in each succeeding variation a different technique is used to vary the material, including ornamentation, figuration, harmonization, rhythmic variation, and so forth. In *Violin Phase* the material is varied by the performer who chooses pitches and rhythms from a composite set of the same material overlaid at different time lags. He doesn't add anything; he merely takes what's already there. I don't think that ever happened in music before. It's similar in a way to one of the principles of orchestration, the doubling of a melody or accentuating certain points in the music with the addition of other instruments. These techniques are used mainly for coloration, emphasis, and the expansion of the sound volume. In *Violin Phase*, the technique of extraction and creating new material from the overlays of two or more sets of the same material, in real time, as it is happening, is a new structural idea.

Drumming

LE VAISSEAU ARGO — THE SHIP ARGO

A frequent image: that of the ship *Argo* (luminous and white), each piece of which the Argonauts gradually replaced, so that they ended with an entirely new ship, without having to alter either its name or its form. This ship *Argo* is highly useful: it affords the allegory of an eminently structural object, created not by genius, inspiration, determination, evolution, but by two modest actions (which cannot be caught up in any mystique of creation): *substitution* (one part replaces the other, as in a paradigm) and *nomination* (the name is in no way linked to the stability of the parts): by dint of combinations made within one and the same name, nothing is left of the origin. *Argo* is an object with no other cause than its name, with no other identity than its form.

— Roland Barthes, *Roland Barthes*, pg. 46

The *Argo* was the ship Jason sailed in quest of the Golden Fleece. What happens if you gradually replace all the planks in the hull? Is it the same ship?

Drumming is a large-scale work for a large ensemble of drummers, singers, and players of mallet instruments. It lasts an hour and a half and sums up Reich's musical thinking up to that time (1972). There are four basic design elements in *Drumming*: the construction of rhythmic patterns by substituting beats for rests and rests for beats; the gradual transitions from one section to another by extremely slow fade-ins and fade-outs, so gradual that one doesn't know the exact moment that one section begins or the other ends; the occasional use of the singing voice to imitate and reinforce instrumental sounds; and phasing techniques as he had developed them in earlier works. But the most salient characteristic of *Drumming* is the assembling and disassembling of the following twelve-beat rhythmic pattern:

Drumming *by Steve Reich, 1973.*

It starts with a single note. A second is added, a third, and so on, until the complete pattern is constructed. It is then simply disassembled, using the reverse process.

The structure has nothing to do with totalitarian political controls imposed from above, but is closely related to yoga control of the breath and mind from within. The kind of attention that mechanical playing calls for is something we should do more of. And the human "expressive" activity, which is assumed to be innately human, and associated with improvisation and similar liberties, is what we could do less of now. Let's think about that.

Burdocks

A burdock is a thistle of the family *Arctium*. It can grow to two or three feet in height, has an edible root (sometimes used for medicinal purposes), and burrs on top. (We've had yarrow stalks, we might as well have burdocks.) The burrs have little hooks and loops on the ends of them made for attaching to whatever passes by them, in order to spread their seeds. They were the inspiration for Velcro. Tolstoy loved the burdock plant. He said it inspired him to write; it clung to life in the most inhospitable places.

Christian Wolff organized a little festival at his farm in Vermont in 1971. He called it the *Burdocks Festival*. There were no posters, no money, just friends gathering together to make music. It was wonderful. *Burdocks*, a large-scale work in ten parts for several orchestras, came from around this time. There are sections for professional musicians and other parts for unskilled players. You can play as many parts as you want. You may choose a director, or form a committee, or hold a meeting to decide which parts to play and who will play them. There's no conductor.

Section II is graphically notated, consisting of two three-by-five grids. The vertical lines describe simultaneity of attack. Certain players give downbeats (cues); anyone can signal a release.

Section V is for more accomplished players. The notation includes what looks like wheels with spokes sticking out of them. I have often thought of these as the burdocks that would be cues for other players, but they simply partition off spaces in which players may play.

Section III simply asks each player to make about five hundred and eleven sounds, each one different. This is a reference to La Monte Young's *Arabic Numeral (Any Integer) for Henry Flynt* (also known as *X for Henry Flynt*) during which a single sound is repeated without intentional variation many times. It is often played by pianists as a series of tone clusters. David Tudor performed it at Darmstadt in 1961, however, by hitting a cymbal on the floor with a drumstick over three hundred times. I was present at that concert. The audience was shocked that a pianist of Tudor's renown would get down on the floor and do such a thing. Pierre Boulez was standing on a chair looking on incredulously. What is different here is that Christian asks a number of players to vary a single sound intentionally. Finding five hundred or so variations of a single sound is a daunting if not impossible task. Christian doesn't actually specify that all five hundred sounds be produced from a single source, but even if you used more than one it would still be a difficult task. In *X for Henry Flynt* one performer discovers the differences in the sounds immediately after he has heard them; in *Burdocks* each player imagines them beforehand, then discovers whether or not he has achieved what he imagined.

In 1965 Andy Warhol produced a 23″ x 22″ offset lithograph of seventy S & H Green Stamps. Green Stamps were given out by the thousands when you bought items in a supermarket, for example. You pasted them in booklets. If you accumulated enough of them you could get a blender. John Cage loved them. Warhol was trying to show the mass repetition in American culture and that everything was the same. But if you looked close enough at each stamp in the grid you could see minute differences in the printing. A dot in the lower left corner, for example, might be slightly darker than another and so forth. It was fascinating to examine a single image with tiny differences.

Number IX may be performed by unskilled players. Each player chooses from one to three fairly quiet sounds. Using one of these at a time, he or she plays as simultaneously as possible with the next sound of the player nearest him or her; then with the next sound of the next nearest player; then with the next nearest after her, and so forth, until he or she has played with all the players in her orchestra. The score suggests a contradictory set of movements: one's sounds stay in place but their connections move out and away with the sounds of others in an allover pattern.

Performers often suggest imposing simple structural ideas on this piece, for example, starting on one side of the room and moving the sounds across to the other side. That's a more specific spatial idea in which the sounds move only in one direction. But that's not what the instructions imply. Christian wants the sounds to move outward from their sources. If you are sitting in the middle of the group your sounds will of course stay there but your connections will move outward in all directions to the far reaches of the group. If you are on the left side your sounds will connect with everyone to your right and vice versa. The sounds remain in their place but the cues come from all over—left and right, back and front, and so forth. When little is given in the form of a score or instructions, performers often, out of anxiety perhaps, impose their own ideas of structure upon these pieces. They feel that there is not enough there; something is missing. Rather than simply doing what is asked and plumbing the depth of the idea, they add a separate layer of structure. Christian puts you in an extremely complex situation, one that is virtually impossible to execute. With so many people how can one hear after the first few sounds what is the next nearer? You have to guess, or have superhuman hearing acuity. The sounds are supposed to spread out through the group. It's like a living organism. If we're attentive enough we might learn something about the growths of natural structures.

Exercises

Heterophony is defined as the simultaneous playing or singing of two or more versions of a melody. It is most often related to folk music or to music that is uncultivated, that is, not composed or performed by musicians trained in universities or music conservatories. The singers or players don't try to stay together but are more concerned with expressing their own music in their own way. They sing or play independently of one another. What happens is accidental or coincidental. We used to call it "primitive" music.

Since 1973 Christian Wolff has composed a series of works called *Exercises*. They are basically made up of single melodic lines, scalar in nature. They are often for any number of instruments. He doesn't specify what clefs to play in. A clef (from the French word for "key") is a symbol that occurs at the beginning of a piece of music indicating what notes occupy the lines and spaces on a five-line staff. The G, or treble, clef tells the player that the note G above middle C occurs on the second line going up from the bottom of the staff; the F, or bass, clef tells the player that the note F below middle C occupies the second line down from the top. The treble clef is usually used by the higher instruments or voices — soprano voice, violin, oboe, and flute; the bass clef by bass voice, cellos, trombones, and tuba. There are several other clefs but the bass and treble are the most common in use today. The invention of clefs gives Western music notation enormous flexibility. In *Exercises* each player reads the clef that is in the range of his or her voice or instrument.

When two instruments play the same line in two different clefs, say the treble and bass, the intervals of major and minor sixths predominate. A note sitting on the middle line of the staff indicates a B in the treble clef but a D in the bass clef. Not counting the octave in between, B and D outline the interval of a major sixth. On the other hand a note sitting in the first space of the treble clef indicates an F but an A in the bass clef outlining a minor sixth. This is due to the structure of the five-line staff.

By not notating rhythm Christian generates unexpected and complex simultaneities and jagged rhythms. At faster tempos the players move out of sync in large proportions; at slower tempos the jaggedness is on a more microscopic level. Attacks and decays of unison notes are closer together, creating timbral differences rather than rhythmic ones. Wolff is drawn to this compositional technique because of its economy and indeterminate nature. The listener focuses on two musical styles: one monophonic (the flow of a single one-line melody), the other polyphonic (created when the line breaks up into two or more strands). He or she waits expectedly for players to jump forward or lag behind the others.

13
PROSE

Stones

Christian Wolff went to England in the Seventies. The most interesting musical things were happening in art schools, not music schools. So he made a collection of pieces for art students. Since most of them couldn't read music he wrote the instructions in prose. In *Stones* he says:

> Make sounds out of stones using a number of sizes and kinds and colors. For the most part, discreetly, sometimes in rapid sequence. For the most part striking stones with stones, but also stones on other surfaces, inside the open head of a drum, for instance. Do not break anything.

Stones is an invitation to open your ears to the sounds of stones. You can think about collecting them either in a haphazard way or take more time and care. You can go looking for stones at the beach or in a quarry. Many performers simply pick up their stones wherever they can find them. If everybody lives in close proximity to each other and simply grabs what they can on their way to the rehearsal or performance, then all the stones will sound similar. All the stones will have come from the same place. The performance will have a monolithic texture. That's fine, I suppose.

Poem for Chairs, Tables, Benches, Etc.

During the summer of 1961, Frederic Rzewski and I visited the Summer Music Course in Darmstadt, Germany. We had just arrived and were walking through the cafeteria when we noticed a group of people pushing chairs and tables around the floor, making scraping and bumping noises. I didn't know what was going on. Later I learned that it was a performance of La Monte Young's *Poem for Chairs, Tables, Benches, Etc.* The original score, written in prose, is very complicated: it includes random number tables, counting out numbers, putting them in a hat, taking certain ones out, deciding how many events you're going to do, determining the time length of the piece, in quarters of seconds if necessary. It's almost impossible to understand. La Monte gives you a task to accomplish, to make a piece whose durations and overall time length are determined by chance operations.

I called La Monte last night and told him we were having a difficult time deciphering the instructions. He told me to forget the instructions, that he simply wanted the players to push the objects around, making continuous sounds. I said we thought we'd do it in the World Music Hall. He asked, What kind of a floor does it have? I said it has a wooden floor. He said he didn't like wooden floors; they're too smooth, the sounds just go "shhh." So Matt Lee and I went over to the World Music Hall to check out the floor. It's a parquet floor, so it's not exactly smooth. I never thought I'd be talking about floors in a course on music, but you have to because that's where the sounds are made. We borrowed a couple of chairs from various offices in the Music Department and spent an hour or so pushing them across the World Music Hall floor. We got beautiful results. La Monte had warned me not simply to allow the students to bring any old thing to the performance. He insisted that they know their instructions before they start playing. You don't want the audience to get the idea that you're learning on the job. You can't show up at the concert and encounter a problem. You will have solved that problem beforehand. Let's all go over to the World Music Hall and experiment.

14
THE PIANO

A Valentine Out of Season

In 1938 John Cage invented the prepared piano. The story goes that while he was teaching at the Cornish School in Seattle he needed percussion sounds for a dance piece he was working on. Having only a piano available, and limited space, he turned the piano into a percussion orchestra. Cage had studied with Henry Cowell, who had experimented with playing inside the piano, plucking and muting the strings with his hands. In Cowell's *The Banshee*, all the sounds are made on the strings themselves, and in *The Aeolian Harp*, one hand silently depresses the keys while the other strums the strings inside. In one work he even went so far as to move a darning egg up and down a string to produce harmonic glissandos. Cowell was also the inventor of the tone cluster, a group of adjacent notes on the piano played by the whole hand, fist or even the forearm. He developed a way of notating them exactly. He published a wonderful book in 1930, *New Musical Resources*, which is filled with fascinating ideas about music, acoustics, rhythmic systems, and so forth.

For some time Cage had been interested in percussion sounds as a way to extricate himself from harmony, tonality, and melody, as they dominated Western music. Drums, cymbals, gongs, as well as found instruments, such as brake drums and tin cans, make noisy, rich, beautiful sounds. In a few instances, found percussion has been used in earlier music: Verdi used a blacksmith's anvil in *Il Trovatore* (the famous *Anvil Chorus*) and Schoenberg calls for clanking chains in *A Survivor from Warsaw*. Audiences seem to accept unusual sounds so long as they're in the percussion section.

If you look back into the early twentieth century, you discover that the piano had already begun to be used for its percussive effects, rather than as a harmonic and melodic instrument. Bartok's *Allegro Barbaro* (1911) consists of almost unremitting hammered piano sounds, whose sharp attacks give the piano a particularly percussive sound. And who can forget the percussive use of the piano in Stravinsky's *Symphony in Three Movements* (1945). It's an unforgettable sound image. So it was only one step further to change the nature of the piano entirely. Cage did this by inserting various materials between the piano strings. He simply went inside the instrument and inserted coins, screws, bolts, pencil erasers, and other objects between the strings, radically altering their sounds.

Cage wrote *A Valentine Out of Season* for his wife, Xenia, in 1944. It's a four-minute work in three movements. He uses only nine notes: B-flat, D, E-flat, F, G-flat, G, A, B and C, forming a scale not heard in Western Music. All the notes are prepared.

Most tones on a grand piano are produced by three strings, tuned to (almost) the same pitch. That's to give it more power. You depress a piano key, causing a hammer to strike the three strings at once. If you insert some material between all three strings, the resulting sound will be muted. If you prepare only two of them, leaving the other free, the resulting sound will be half-muted and half-normal. You get two sounds with one preparation. If you depress the soft pedal, however, the hammer will hit only two strings, so only a muted sound, for example, will be heard. In *Valentine*, Cage uses weather stripping, pennies, bolts, wood, rubber, and slit bamboo. Each material creates a different sound.

Cage specifies each preparation in the score: rubber for the B-flat; weather stripping and pennies for the D and E-flat; weather stripping and a large bolt for the F; slit bamboo and wood for the

G-flat; bolts for the G, A, B, and C. On the D and E-flat, weather stripping and pennies are inserted between all 3 strings; on the F, weather stripping is inserted between the first two strings, a large bolt between the second and third strings. Cage is specific about where on the string the preparation is to be made. For example, the rubber on the B-flat is placed 5⅞ inches from the damper. It's that exact. He must have tried these out and found they produced the best effect. Later on, Cage discovered that no two instruments are alike and he couldn't count on the same preparation producing the same result. So he accepted the differences that came with each performance. While the preparations were exactly determined, the results were not. This was a first step to his acceptance of indeterminacy.

Frederic Rzewski told me a funny story about the prepared piano. He was in Walter Piston's composition class at Harvard in the late Fifties. One day Piston asked the class what was new in music. Rzewski answered that the prepared piano was especially interesting. Piston asked him to demonstrate it. Frederic proceeded to insert coins between the strings of certain pitches. Piston, in telling about this later remarked: "Why, there must have been almost forty cents in that piano!" I told that story to Cage who howled with laughter and made me tell it over and over again.

Here is a story that Richard K. Winslow tells about Cage and the prepared piano. In 1952 Cage wrote to Winslow, who was on the music faculty at Wesleyan, and said he'd like to come and give a concert with David Tudor. An announcement came out advertising a concert by "John Cage and David Tudor, Skrewball Pianists." The publicist must have thought Spike Jones was coming. The concert took place in the chapel. In those days you had to go to chapel a certain number of times a week, but if there were a cultural event, you could go to that instead. You could choose either church or a poetry reading. (Personally, I'd take the poetry reading.) The place was packed. As soon as they heard the music, young men (Wesleyan was a men-only college then) were running over to their fraternities telling their friends to come hear this crazy music. The first half consisted of pieces of Stockhausen, Boulez, and Christian Wolff. During the intermission John invited the audience to come up on stage and watch him prepare the piano. Dick said that people jumped out of the balcony and ran across the tops of the pews to get to the stage, then crowded around Cage to see what was going on. That was the first performance by Cage at Wesleyan.

Music for Amplified Toy Pianos

Performing Cage's music is not supposed to make you feel restricted. It's supposed to enable you to learn something, to open up rather than repeat something that you do from personal taste or habit. One of Cage's ideas was that music should be about discovery, not about the repetition of habits or personal taste. I remember performing Cage's *Music for Amplified Toy Pianos* (1960) once with David Tudor. It had an indeterminate score. I was very careful to make my determinations by overlaying transparencies as accurately as possible because I wanted the experience of performing a work of Cage's in the spirit in which he imagined it. I timed everything precisely. We started playing. And all of a sudden we both stopped. We both got to a point where our chance operations gave us a minute of silence. In those days a minute of silence on a concert stage was unbearable. When have you ever been at a concert when the orchestra stopped playing for a whole minute? I was terribly embarrassed and I thought I was a fraud. I had been trained to make and play work that has drama, that moves from point A to point B, from one key to another, which has melody and harmony, things of that sort. All of a sudden two people playing wonderful raucous sounds on enormously amplified toy pianos both stop and there's a hole in the sound.

In John Barth's novel, *Once Upon a Time*, he describes the "curve" of classical dramatic action as a non-equilateral triangle where *ab* represents the "rising action" or incremental complication of some conflict; *b* the climactic "epiphany" or reversal of fortune; and *bc* the denouement, or resolution of dramatic tension. The line *ab* has a longer rise time than *bc*'s descent. In Greek drama the action builds up to the climax, and once the climax is achieved, coming off the climax is not as long. John Cage has spent his life exploring formal structures that don't do that, but do the unexpected instead. By using chance, he enables you to eliminate or forego all those habitual ideas that you have and to discover something different. When Tudor and I got to that minute of silence it just was so wonderful to have an empty hole there. It was like the negative space in a Barbara Hepworth sculpture. Who says you can't do that? Why isn't that a beautiful proportion? It just means you stop soon after you start. You sometimes do that in life, don't you? It's just a different structural proportion. It has nothing to do with fulfilling human desire. It runs counter to the Wagnerian climax, where you build up one phrase, then the next phrase is a little longer, and another a little longer still, then there's the climax and the whole orchestra is playing, the soprano is singing at the top of her lungs, fulfilling the expectation, fulfilling your needs. John Cage is interested in letting sounds be themselves and be expressive in their own right. If a performer wants so many loud sounds here and is determined to make them simply because she wants to do it, she's being self-indulgent and that's not what this piece is about. So even though these are sometimes ambiguous instructions, if you intend to perform in a spirit of trying to make those particular versions as accurate as possible—then, if you do make a mistake, for Mr. Cage it is not a mistake. It's a matter of good intentions. If a terrible singer's intentions are good, Cage will accept the performance. If a wonderful singer uses a Cage piece in order to bring attention to herself, that's not in the spirit of the music.

Piece for Four Pianos

The score for Morton Feldman's *Piece for Four Pianos* (1957) is only one page long. There are seventy-five events, including chords, single tones, rests, and a couple of figurations. The pitches are notated, but there's no time signature, no rhythm. What's astonishing about it is that all four players play from the same score. Let's read the instructions; they're very simple:

> The first sound with all pianos is made simultaneously. Durations for each sound are chosen by the performer. All beats are slow and not necessarily equal. Dynamics are low with a minimum of attack. Grace notes should not be played too quickly. Numbers between sounds are equal to silent beats.

By specifying low dynamics and no attack, Feldman is establishing his own special sound world. If you've ever seen a spectrogram of a piano attack, you'll notice a noisy spike at the beginning, followed by a dip in the sound, then a slow rise in loudness before the sound decays to silence. The sound quickly fades into a purer waveform, resembling a sine wave with no overtones. Due to slightly imprecise tunings among the strings, slow audible beating occurs, causing a slow swelling sound as the sound waves coincide. It's called the aftersound and it's what gives the piano tone its distinctive shape. Now if you mitigate the attack and keep the loudness level low, you remove most of the noise, leaving a more pure sinusoidal waveform; you're changing the sound color, the sound of the piano. It sounds almost electronic. It has a Morton Feldman sound.

I remember listening to a series of recordings in which the attacks of different musical instruments were cut off. By removing them, it was more difficult to identify the instruments. Then, as the overtones were filtered out, the instruments became indistinguishable from one another. I never heard Morty talk about acoustics, but he did a remarkable thing by transforming the piano sound and making it entirely his own. It was uncanny.

Historically, grace notes are supposed to be played quickly; they're not functional and exist out of the time domain of the work. They steal time from the note they are supposed to grace. Feldman notates them in the normal manner, then instructs you not to play them quickly, that is, not the way they were intended to be played. A performer will play a grace note differently than a normal one, more lightly. And, in *Piece for Four Pianos*, because the pianist will think of it as an ornament even though there's no tone to be ornamented, the sound will be different because of it. By telling the players not to play them too fast he's giving you the feeling of how to play the piece physically. It's as if he's a painter suggesting a certain type of brush stroke.

In a classical sonata the listener knows where he or she is most of the time. The composer may try to fool him or her by aiming for one key and at the last moment going somewhere else. Beethoven loved doing this. But in classical music the structural points are clear. In *Piece for Four Pianos*, despite the redundancy provided by four pianists playing the same music, the listener tends to lose his or her bearings; after awhile he or she doesn't recognize the repetitions. Feldman, however, composes stopping points along the way where everybody catches up. There are four such oases where the same sounds are repeated three, four, and five times each. They are distributed more or less evenly throughout the piece. Chances are a pianist won't be so far behind that she won't sooner or later come together with the others. Since there are four pianists, there'll be fifteen, twenty, and twenty-five repetitions of each event. They're beautiful moments. They aren't climaxes; they're confluences. In conventional music climaxes, simplification comes after complexity. Think of that spectacular moment in Bartok's *Music for Strings, Percussion, and Celesta* where the instruments open up to bare fifths and octaves after a tortuous fugal rise in emotion. It's different with Feldman. The same event is repeated at the moment the listeners (and the players) find themselves lost, spread out too far apart. Repeating the same event until everybody catches up simplifies the situation. To be sure, there's plenty of repetition in Mozart and Beethoven. Motives get repeated over and over, but they're used as building blocks to form phrases, longer themes, and larger structures. In Feldman, the repetitions don't go anywhere. I suppose we could call his music static, but we don't need adjectives, do we?

The four pianists all play exactly the same music. They don't really interact with one another in the way that jazz players do, for example. As you're playing you hear the other person, obviously, but you don't slow down or speed up because of what the other person's doing. You're playing the music at your own speed. What you hear around you, in some inscrutable way, influences how you play, but that's not a part of this piece. It's not interactive music. Feldman uses the words, "echo," "reflection," and "reverberation" when he talks about this piece.

Have you noticed how many contemporary buildings are made of glass? You see reflections of passersby and the buildings around them more than the buildings themselves. Reflection and repetition take the place of the more dramatic, assertive structures of the past. What a different idea!

The art critic Harold Rosenberg described American painting as undeveloped landscape instead of the cultivated gardens of Western Europe, and described how colonial sharpshooters, hiding behind rocks and trees, picked off the British soldiers marching in strict ranks through the forest. They didn't understand the terrain. We could think of the form of *Piece for Four Pianos* as different terrain.

We played *Piece for Four Pianos* at Wesleyan several years ago with Feldman and three Wesleyan pianists, including faculty member Jon Barlow. During rehearsals Feldman remarked to Jon that he played like a philosopher. He meant it as praise. For several years afterwards I would hear that we had a pianist up at Wesleyan who played like a philosopher.

The Well-Tuned Piano

The title, *The Well-Tuned Piano*, is a reference to Bach's great keyboard work, *The Well-Tempered Clavier*. It consists of two books of twenty-four preludes and fugues, one each in all twelve major and twelve minor keys. In Bach's time, clavier meant any keyboard instrument. Nowadays his music is usually played on a piano. To temper is to soften or modify. In music it refers to altering the tuning of a keyboard instrument so that it can play in several keys, each of which sounds similar to the other. Before Bach's time (1685–1750) there were many types of tuning. The Pythagorean (c. 550 B.C.) scale was constructed by stacking perfect fifths one upon another until all twelve chromatic pitches were accounted for. This was called the circle of fifths. It was a pretty good tuning system — the fifths were in perfect tune — except that when it came full circle, the final pitch was a little higher than the original. That's because a perfect fifth has 702 cents (100 cents per semitone). Eleven times 702 equals 7,722. This small surplus of 22 cents is called the Pythagorean Comma. (John Cage wrote the *Freeman Etudes* for solo violin in Pythagorean tuning and in which the Comma plays a role.) Mean Tone temperament, which was in use around 1500, was based on slightly flattened fifths — about 697 cents each — but produced more or less pure major thirds. It was useful for playing in a few closely related keys but as soon as you roamed to distantly related ones the flat fifths took their toll and the intervals became more and more out of tune. Suffice it to say that in Bach's time (1685–1750) tuning systems were in a state of transition.

In the natural world every musical tone consists of a fundamental — that's the tone you hear — and a virtually infinite series of overtones or partials that sound faintly above it. The overtones occur in a specific order above the fundamental: the octave, perfect fifth, perfect fourth, major third, minor third and so forth. The intervals get smaller as you get higher. If you number them you can easily see that they may be expressed in whole number ratios: 2:1; 3:2; 4:3; 5:4; 6:5; 7:6, and so forth. As long as you tune intervals in these simple low number ratios you will get a natural form of tuning called Just Intonation. Singers and players of non-fixed instruments such as the violin and flute naturally play in Just Intonation (or something close to it). Even though the overtones or partials are virtually inaudible, performers hear them subliminally; they intuitively adjust their pitches to the series as they go along. A problem arises with keyboard and fretted instruments whose pitches are fixed. As long as the instrument is tuned to the overtones of a certain fundamental you can play in Just Intonation; but if you want to play the same music in a different key, starting on a different pitch—this is called transposition—your intervals won't be the same size and your melody, for example, will sound distorted. Think of a totem pole, which has a monolithic structure. Pretend that the images get smaller as you go up the pole. There is no way to recreate the same size images starting a third the way up the pole; for example, you would have to begin again with a new bottom image (fundamental). Pauline Oliveros's orchestral work, *Tashi Gomang* (Tibetan for "good" or "fortunate flying," in the sense of meditation), uses a single series. Starting on Low E at 41 cycles per second she generates sixty-four overtones above it. The players are asked to improvise on certain notated pitches of the series. To help the players she gives images for each section: *Lake*, *Brisk Wind*, *Yellow*, *Water*, and so forth.

One way to get around the tuning problem is to make the distances between pitches equal; then what sounds one way in one key will sound exactly the same in another. This form of tuning is called Equal Temperament. Our modern pianos are tuned this way. We may have lost the beauty of natural tuning but we've gained the flexibility to design large musical structures in which the listener is taken from one tonal region to another. You can play the same music starting on any key and it will sound virtually the same. In a Beethoven symphony, for example, the drama consists in taking you from one key to another. This ability to change key suggests travel and development, coinciding with Western countries' era of colonization. Every sonata form movement has a development section in which the composer embroiders the musical material in the first two themes. Western classical music gave up the purity of natural intervals for that flexibility. Just as Bach's *The Well-Tempered Clavier* is a virtuoso showpiece for a newly developing tempered tuning system (not Equal Temperament exactly) La Monte Young's *The Well-Tuned Piano* is a showpiece for what is called Extended Just Intonation.

Young, Terry Riley, and other composers in the 1960s wanted music to go back to a natural state. La Monte took inspiration from the study of acoustics as well the music of other cultures, particularly India. In fact, for many years he was a devoted student of Pran Nath, a Sufi singer of uncanny ability. Myths have grown up around his singing. One story is that his tuning was so accurate that he could make pictures fall off the wall or curtains ripple. Young decided he would make works based on a natural tuning derived from the overtone series. It was beautiful to look back and do that. It was something our culture needed.

Young generates an overtone series for *The Well-Tuned Piano* by imagining a fundamental tone, E-flat, ten octaves below human audibility. What an amazing idea! He then chooses interval ratios from high up on that series. The reason he uses number ratios is because they are exactly repeatable. Any two tones in a ratio of 3:2 will give you a perfect fifth every time it is played. The ear hears that interval the same way every time. But if one of the tones slips even a little bit the ratio is no longer 3:2, say 3.001:2. It will then take an extremely long time for exactly the same interval to repeat exactly. Since the intervals on the equal tempered piano are out of tune, both squeezed and expanded, only the octaves repeat exactly. The chance that two repetitions of the same interval will be in the same phase relationship is virtually impossible. The only way you could hear the interval repeated exactly is to listen a lifetime until the pitches come back into phase. This concept led La Monte to consider making works that are timeless. In fact, he thinks of his total oeuvre as one huge piece. He is not interested in chance, he's interested in control. He wants you to hear the same interval exactly the same way over and over again because the pitches will impinge on the cochlea in the ear the same way over and over again producing a certain psychic state that he aims for.

To do this he procured a Bösendorfer Imperial piano. It's made in Europe and is larger than a nine-foot Steinway. It's more resonant and has six more keys on its lower end. It takes La Monte a couple of months to tune it. He uses an electronic tuner but works a lot by ear. He asserts that he can get around the overtone series, that is, hear slight differences in tunings. Once he tunes the piano, it can't be moved or it'll go out of tune — like any piano — so he requires a semi-permanent space for it and plenty of time to work on the tuning. There's an article by Kyle Gann that describes the tunings.

In a certain sense, *The Well-Tuned Piano* is a work for prepared piano. Young modifies certain aspects of the piano. First he puts in a bar of felt and wood that allows the hammers to hit a single string. He even shaves the hammers so that they hit the string in the same place each time they strike it. He makes sure that the string is sounded at the same place each time. He also inserts bars of felt that are in the shape of cones, so he can raise the dampers on only certain strings, so that when he plays, only those strings resonate.

Young's performances are characterized by repetition. He does this because the pitches that are derived by rational numbers sound exactly the same each time they are played. He feels that by repeating something exactly he can give you the specific feeling of the interval each and every time. It's completely opposite the ideas of John Cage. You can imagine that Cage is delighted by the slight changes in intonation on the modern piano. He wants you to hear slight differences. In a typical performance Young explores regions that contain different sets of intervals. Each one has a romantic name—*The Moonlight Sonata Passage*, *The Interlude of the Wind and the Waves*, *Sunlight Filtering Through Leaves*, *The Subtractive Variations of the Theme of the Magic Chord*, *The Theme of the Dawn of the Eternal Time*. He improvises for about five hours, moving from one region to another. *The Well-Tuned Piano* doesn't have a narrative structure; there are simply a series of regions that the performer moves through. Kyle Gann has pointed out the irony that one of the most important works for the piano in the twentieth century has no written score.

La Monte's piano sounds are so rich that when he plays a series of notes in a rapid *tremolo* style, you can hear clouds of sound surrounding the instrument. You hear the waves physically vibrating in the space. If one or more notes beat against each other, that is, if they're tuned so close together you can hear audible beats when their cycles coincide, he will play at the speed of that beating. The beats tell him how fast to play. You can hear the tuning as physical phenomena; they shimmer. You have to be in the space, listening to a large Bösendorfer with the lid up, to experience this. *The Well-Tuned Piano* is one of the first pieces of music in which the tuning is the score. It can only be played on that piano; it couldn't be played on a Steinway. The Bösendorfer is shaped like a regular piano. The German word for grand piano is Flügel (wing).

Speaker Swinging

Several years ago Gordon Monahan came to Wesleyan to perform his *Speaker Swinging* in the basketball court in the old gym.

Three performers stood on pedestals and swung loudspeakers in circular motions on long ropes and speaker cables for about forty-five minutes. Sine waves flowed from the speakers. As the speakers spun around the performers' heads the pitches of the waves rose and fell slightly because of the Doppler effect. You know that when a police car speeds by with its siren sounding its tone descends as the vehicle gets farther and farther away or rises when it approaches. That's because the waves are getting compressed and elongated relative to the observer. If you measure the rate of change you can estimate the speed of the police car. It's a remarkable phenomenon. It was named after Austrian mathematician Christian Andreas Doppler (1803–1853).

Piano Mechanics

Gordon returned a few years later and performed *Piano Mechanics*, a solo work in nine movements, each of which explores a specific acoustic characteristic of the grand piano. I'm emphasizing piano pieces in which the instrument actually sounds different than other piano pieces. I'm eliminating a lot of wonderful pieces and concentrating on those in which the composer has actually changed the sound of the instrument. For example, John Cage prepared the piano by inserting objects between the strings; Henry Cowell stroked the strings inside the piano; La Monte Young very carefully tunes a special piano.

The story goes that Monahan was playing piano one night in a rock band. In one piece he was loudly pounding single notes and clusters in the lowest register of the instrument. When the piece was over the other guys in the band asked him if he heard what had been happening while he was playing. He replied that he hadn't because he had earmuffs on, the music was so loud. They told him that the piano jumped into a mode of vibration, and that the strings were sympathetically resonating in a most violent manner. It was if the instrument heated up and started boiling. It was an astonishing sound. It was like alchemy. Other sections of *Piano Mechanics* explore other phenomena. In Part 8 the player trills in the upper reaches of the keyboard loudly enough so as to produce difference tones. In another the player hits the keys so hard you hear the sound of wood. Composer Daniel Wolf says that even though the piece is completely acoustic it sounds prepared or enhanced by electronic means. He goes on to say "the techniques used are musically naïve, being closer to the explorations made by patient children when left alone at the keyboard." Coincidentally, in German composer Helmut Lachenmann's piano piece, *Kinderspiele* (*Child Play*) the pianist strikes the top keys in ways similar to Monahan but in simple, almost banal rhythms such as a child would invent. In fact Lachenmann wrote the piece for his seven-year-old child.

Canon X

Conlon Nancarrow fought on the socialist side in the Spanish Civil War and was not allowed back into the United States. So he lived in Mexico City most of his adult life. Throughout his life he has composed over fifty pieces for player piano. You know what a player piano is? Before we had digital pianos, virtually every home had a player piano. You could put in a roll that was punched full of holes. Powered by foot pedals, which send air into a complex mechanism, a device would see the holes on the roll and play the keys on the piano. You would sit at the piano, pump it with your feet, and "play" the popular tunes of the day. Nancarrow was drawn to this instrument because he could create the most outlandish rhythmic and melodic figurations at crazy speeds. It can also make perfectly gradual accelerandos and decelerandos. This gives the pieces a superhuman and witty quality that delights and astounds audiences. In Study No. 21, *Canon X*, one "hand" starts high up on the keyboard and slows down, the other starts low and speeds up. They cross in the middle. Nancarrow maintains total logarithmic control of the tempo.

In 1989 Nancarrow wrote *2 Canons*, a work in conventional notation for pianist Ursula Opens. It has all the rhythmic complexity of his player piano works. When Ursula plays it, it looks easy. Actually, there is a third canon for Ursula that asks the performer to play in four tempos at the same time. Nancarrow was thought to have deleted it from his list of works but it has mysteriously resurfaced and has been played by another pianist. It goes to show how something impossible to execute becomes possible once a wonderful pianist is able to cut it. David Tudor did that with early piano sonatas of Pierre Boulez. They were considered too difficult to play. Tudor came along, played them perfectly, and after that they became part of virtuoso pianists' repertoire. It's like breaking the four-minute mile. In 1954 Roger Bannister ran a mile in 3:59.4 seconds. Soon after other runners came along and followed suit.

15

LONG STRING INSTRUMENT

Ellen Fullman said something beautiful about her piece, *The Long String Instrument* (1980). She said that the activity of its composition had become her personal music school. It led her to read and study as the information she sought got put to use in very practical ways, and that the piece is a microcosm for the history of music. Why did she say it's a microcosm of the history of music? One of the earliest examples of writing we've got about music is by Pythagoras, a mathematician in fifth-century B.C. Greece. He invented the monochord, a single string, which when plucked and bowed allows one to observe its modes of vibration. Pythagoras was interested in the nature of sound, making him the first experimental composer.

The first thing one observes is that the string vibrates as a whole. You can see it moving up and down its entire length. The sound it produces as it vibrates as a whole is the fundamental pitch. That's the tone you hear and identify. Its pitch is determined by the tautness, weight, mass, and length of the string. Any mechanical system that moves periodically faster than sixteen times a second makes a musical sound. The pitch of an organ pipe is determined by how long it is; the column of air is vibrating in that length. All things being equal the longer the vibrating medium, the lower the sound; the shorter, the higher. That's why the piccolo sounds higher than the tuba. At the same time the string vibrates as a whole, it vibrates in half, producing a sound an octave higher than the fundamental. The string also vibrates in thirds, fourths, fifths and so on. Each mode of vibration produces a tone that is heard at the same time as the fundamental, but so quietly that you don't hear it individually. You hear it as timbre. That's why musical sounds are so interesting and have such beautiful timbres, they're composed of so many overtones. At first, Ellen worked with long strings in a haphazard way, then she got interested in tunings and trying to figure out what the basic principles were. She was relearning the history of acoustics.

It's difficult to understand how something can vibrate in half at the same time it's vibrating as a whole and in thirds. It's hard to believe that strings vibrate simultaneously in all these ways. The overtones contribute to the timbre of the sound. Just because I move my arm one way, doesn't mean my elbow can't be moving at the same time. There's a myth about basketball superstar Michael Jordan. Some people think that when he's in mid-air he can jump up even higher. That's why he's called "Air Jordan." But that's physically impossible. He would have nothing solid to jump against. They discovered that he simply changes his center of gravity. He can move his body while he's up in the air in a way that makes it seem as if he were jumping higher. Physical systems are hard to explain. Every physics book I've ever read never quite explains these things enough. How can you explain the magic of sound? Every model is too simple. I think the question has to do with whether there are certain innate properties, perhaps universal properties, that have to do with acoustics. I don't think that this phenomenon is ever adequately explained. It just happens.

Several years ago Ellen Fullman did a beautiful performance of *The Long String Instrument* in the old Field House at Wesleyan. She extended her strings all the way down the basketball court. Regulation length for a college court is ninety-four feet so her wire must have been close to that. The strings were tuned to sound boxes positioned under the baskets. During the performance she and an assistant walked forward and back down the court between the strings, stroking them with rosined fingers. The pitch stays the same no matter where they are on the wire but the timbre changes. She tuned the wires by putting clamps at certain points on the wire to shorten the lengths of the strings. It's similar to the way a violinist stops a string. Let's bow any open string. If you stop it with your first finger a perfect fourth above, it produces a harmonic two octaves higher because the sounding part of the string is shorter. A flutist, a wind player, will press a key down shortening the length of the air tube. A brass player does the same thing with valves.

The two performers slowly walked forward and backward as in a dream, stroking the strings on either side of them. Before the concert I asked her how long she was going to play and she said an hour. I thought that seemed too long, but it wasn't. Everyone was mesmerized.

Music on a Long Thin Wire

The idea for *Music on a Long in Wire* (1977) came out of a physics class at Wesleyan I taught with physicist John Trefny. We set up a modern version of the Pythagorean monochord by extending a wire across the top of a lab table, an electromagnet straddling one end. We began stopping and plucking the string in various ways and observing the modes of vibration. I went home one night and dreamed of an extremely long wire. I dreamed of a wire that reached up to the moon. Do you know the *Running Fence* by Christo? He constructed a fence that ran hundreds of miles across California. Perhaps I was inspired by that work. Anyway, I knew that by greatly extending the length of the wire the result would sound amazing.

I'm not primarily concerned about tuning in *Music on a Long Thin Wire*. I don't try to control it. I simply take the longest length that I can and listen to what happens. I recently installed *Music on a Long Thin Wire* in the Stadtgalerie in Kiel, Germany. It was one hundred and twenty feet long. The gallery space was a quarter of a circle and my wire went across it. There was almost no room for anybody to walk around. You don't know what a quarter of a circle really is until you walk around in it. The architecture was perfectly symmetrical. The wire was extended between two wooden tables. (I specify wooden tables because the sound of wood is beautiful.) I placed wooden bridges with notches cut into them for the wire to fit into, on each table. Contact microphones were embedded in the bridges. These microphones were routed to separate amplifiers and speakers. When the wire vibrated, the microphones picked up the sound in the wood. What made the wire vibrate was an electrical current provided by an audio oscillator. The oscillator is routed into an amplifier, and the amplifier goes into one end of the wire. The other is routed by a long cable to the other side of the amp, forming a loop. A current alone was not enough to make the wire move so I placed a horseshoe magnet over the wire at one end. The magnet creates a flux field across the wire causing it to move. It's like a loudspeaker without a cone. I sent away for a U.S. Navy surplus horseshoe magnet through the Edmund Scientific Catalog. God knows what the Navy did with horseshoe magnets. It weighs about thirty pounds. I have to hide it in my luggage when I bring it over to Europe on an airplane. If they know it's a magnet they won't let me take it, they think it'll throw the plane off course. If they ask me what it is I say it's a sculpture. Sometimes, though, I simply remove one of the poles of the magnet and carry it in another piece of luggage. I don't know the power of the magnet, I just work with it empirically. I simply install it and turn on the amplifier. I find a pitch on the oscillator that makes the wire vibrate. Since the wire is so long it makes wonderful sounds, but more important, they change all of the time because the wire's slack, it's not under tension the way piano strings are. Footsteps, temperature changes, air currents also cause the wire to change. It's a fragile system.

Music on a Long Thin Wire started as a performance piece but I never knew what to tell the players to do. I played it with oscillators. You could change the pitch of the oscillators, and the sound would spectacularly change. But it was too spectacular. It was like playing a giant guitar. I had no language for it. Once you've made a change, then what do you do? Unless you have a musical language, it just doesn't make sense, so I thought it would be mysterious if it just played itself. You could create a system that would play itself. And this is what it's doing. I'm not touching a thing here. I recorded this in darkness up in the rotunda of the U.S. Custom House in New York. I was up there by myself. The wire was ninety feet long. Once I tuned it and raised the volume level I never touched it. I was listening to all of those changes. And I didn't think any thing was really happening. It's not that too much is happening, except overtones come out and you can hear them. There seem to be chords trying to come out. All of sudden this silvery chord appears. I swear to you I never touched it. I recorded four twenty-minute versions for a double long-playing recording. Each side has a different tuning. I made the tunings by ear. I don't remember what pitches I used.

Radial Arcs

British physicist William Duddell was one of the first inventors of electronic music. Quite by accident. In 1899 he was working on a project to try to mitigate the constant sizzling noise made by arc lights, caused by constant sparking between two carbon electrodes. He was unable to eliminate the sound, but he learned that by controlling the electric current of the high-voltage oscillator that caused the sparking, he could vary the tones generated by the sparks. He wired the arc lights to a keyboard, inventing what may have been the first electronic (keyboard) musical instrument. He called these phenomena "singing arcs."

Ron Kuivila's *Radial Arcs*, exhibited as part of the 1988 *Ars Electronica Festival*, Linz, consisted of ninety-six coordinated singing arcs distributed throughout the exhibition space. They were driven by a computer-controlled high voltage oscillator. Wires were extended in radial patterns mirroring the architecture of the Brucknerhaus where it was presented. A bridge was constructed so that the viewer/listener could walk through these lightning fields with relative safety even though 12,000 volts of electricity were shooting around them. Kuivila reduced the size of the work so as to lessen any feeling of violence—the spark gap as bug zapper. However, the fact that the work was constructed using stun gun transformers nonetheless gave it a sinister feeling.

In an earlier installation, *Parallel Lines* (1985), pairs of wires were extended around the room, placed close enough together so sparks, leaping from one wire to another, were generated at various points along their lengths producing hundreds of miniature lightning storms. Spark gaps, defined as spaces between two electrodes across which a discharge of electricity may take place, produce sounds that flows in all directions at once, giving them a mysterious presence.

16

RECORDING

Sferics

Sferics is the shortened term for atmospherics, electromagnetic disturbances in the ionosphere. They're natural radio waves in the audible spectrum caused by electrical storms in the ionosphere. You can't hear them with the naked ear. They're not sound waves, they're radio waves. But they're low enough in frequency that you don't have to transpose them down into the range of human hearing.

Scientists call these phenomena bonks, tweeks, and whistlers. A whistler is a bonk that has been caught by the magnetic flux lines surrounding the earth and actually travels thousands of miles, producing a long descending whistling sound as it does so. Doesn't Thomas Pynchon's *Gravity's Rainbow* open with a scene at a whistler listening station in Africa?

I had done a couple of performances with noisy disc recordings made by astrophysicist Millett Morgan at Dartmouth, but thought it would be wonderful to record them for myself. In 1968 Pauline Oliveros invited me to the University of California at San Diego to record these phenomena. Nobody knew how to do it then. We went out into canyons with homemade radio receivers, trying to avoid electrical hum from power lines. Whenever you're near electric lights or electric power you get a 60-cycle hum that interferes with clear reception. If you could get away from electric power, you'd get a clearer signal. There was nowhere to go in Southern California to get away from electric power. One evening Pauline and I went out to a helicopter launching pad in La Jolla. All we got was the noisy signals of fighter planes taking off for Vietnam from a nearby naval air base. The performance was a disaster.

Years later Ned Sublette recommended *Listening to Radio Energy, Light, and Sound*, a do-it-yourself book by Calvin R. Graf. The author tells you how to make large loop antennas by crossing a couple of strips of wood, cutting notches in them, and winding eighty feet of eighteen-gauge wire around them to form simple but effective antennas. They are powerful enough to receive sferics. I simply plugged the antennas into a battery-operated cassette tape recorder. All I had to do was match the impedance of the antennas with that of the microphone inputs of the recorder.

I drove up to the top of a mountain in Colorado, one night in late August 1980, to get away from power lines. A few weeks before I had called up the Atmospheric Lab in Boulder and asked someone if he thought I would get a stereo effect if I used a pair of antennas instead of only one. He wasn't sure but thought I would have to position them a thousand miles apart. I started to think how to synchronize the signals over such a long distance. I had a friend in Australia. Perhaps we could figure out a way to do it.

I set up my antennas, leaning them up against a couple of bushes, turned on my tape recorder and, lo and behold, I heard sferics as clear as day (night, actually) through a pair of headphones. I discovered that by simply spreading the two antennas twenty or thirty feet apart and aiming them in different directions I could get a beautiful stereo sound field. Every time I changed the tape I would randomly re-orient the antennas, shifting their positions a little, thereby shifting the spatial quality of the stereo field. I got a faint whistler at around 11:30 P.M., then a series of them just before dawn.

A few years later I installed *Sferics* once more in El Morro, New Mexico, as part of an Earth Watch project. We set up a small array of antennas on the top of a mesa. Visitors could come and sit in camp chairs and hear sferics in real time. One night there was a distant lightning storm. You could see lightning and hear loud bonks simultaneously. They were manifestations of the same event. Ionospheric disturbances are happening all the time. The ionosphere lies about eighty to three hundred miles above the earth. It merges with the magnetosphere, part of the Van Allen Belt. It becomes active at night. At dawn it quiets down. It's so beautiful up in the mountains to watch dawn come up as the atmospherics sparse out. It's ironic, too, that you have to go out into the wilderness to make the recording. There's a lovely crunching sound near the end. I have no idea what caused it. It's much more interesting to listen for whistlers in real time than to hear them on tape.

Angels and Insects

There's a beautiful recording of underwater sounds by David Dunn called *Angels and Insects*. Beneath the water's surface are a variety of plants and insects. While the sounds above water are comfortable and familiar those occurring under the surface are shocking. Their alien variety seems unprecedented as if controlled by a mysterious spirit. The minutiae that produced these audible rasps and sputters remain mostly unseen among plants and layers of silt. Each contributes to a sonic universe. The timbres of these sounds are magnificent, a tiny orchestra of percussion players, seemingly intoxicated. Bio-acousticians have hypothesized that every location on earth inhabited by living organisms has a unique acoustical bio-spectrum. They're not just uttering random sounds, there's logic to it. The chorus of sounds that comprise these biospectra may provide information about the dynamics of a resonant ecosystem—I almost said echo system—such that status information about their collective ecology is transmitted to its coexisting organisms. It seems as if they are all informing each other as to what their situation is. David Dunn made these wonderful recordings in freshwater ponds in North America and Africa using underwater microphones. In many instances he has had to lower and slow down the sounds to get them into the human range of audibility. They are simply too high for us to hear. If *Angels and Insects* were a piece of electronic music, you'd be impressed by how beautiful and complex it would be.

A Sound Map of the Hudson River

Annea Lockwood's *A Sound Map of the Hudson River* is such a simple idea. She recorded the sounds of the Hudson River at various points, from its source in the Adirondacks to New York Harbor. I remember hearing portions of this recording on Minnesota Public Radio in the Eighties. There was a festival of New Music America in Minneapolis–Saint Paul, and National Public Radio gave Lockwood fifteen minutes every noon to play her recordings of river sounds. I'd drive from St. Paul to Minneapolis, and turn on the radio to hear the beautiful sound of a river. It was the perfect thing to hear on the radio in Minnesota. There was no advertising, no talking, just fifteen minutes of natural flowing water sound. That's something radio can do, it can be environmental—you just turn your radio on and hear sounds of the environment. In a sense this piece as well as *Sferics* and *Angels and Insects* are permanent installations in the world of nature. Each geographical location provokes a different state of mind. You feel a little bit differently about it. It may be determined by the weather, the terrain. I fish a great deal in Colorado. As you walk the streams, you hear different resonances as the water flows in different places, around sunken logs, under grassy banks, and so forth. It's sonically so rich. There's no music that can emulate that complexity. When people say that noise in music isn't natural, you can point to noise in nature. The waveforms are complex and aperiodic. Nature is very noisy.

17

OPERA

Einstein on the Beach

The first thing you hear in *Einstein on the Beach* is a three-note bass line played on an electric organ. It is repeated over and over again as the audience comes in to the theater. It takes the place of an overture. The notes are A, G, and C, the sixth, fifth and first degrees of a C-major scale. It's a basic Western harmonic cadential figure. Let's take a look at each of the seven degrees of such a scale.

If we step up the white notes on a piano keyboard, starting on C, we get a C-major scale: C, D, E, F, G, A, B, and C. If we construct triads (chords consisting of two thirds stacked one upon the other) on each of the seven degrees we discover that I (C), IV (F) and V (G) are major triads, having major thirds (two whole steps) on the bottom, minor thirds (one whole, one half step) on top. II (D), III (E), and VI (A) are minor triads, minor thirds on the bottom, major thirds on top. VII (B) is a diminished triad, consisting of two minor thirds. I, IV, and V are strong triads, by virtue of their structure (major) and their roots (bottom tones) that appear early in the overtone series on C. I is the fundamental; V, the third overtone; IV, the fourth. II, III, and VI are relatively weak, relating to the stronger triads. II and VI share two tones with IV and I. III shares two tones with I and V. VII is unstable—it shares tones with V, II, and IV. It can't stand by itself, it has to go somewhere, usually to I. The strongest cadential figure in Western harmony is IV, V, I. By substituting VI for IV, Philip is substituting a weaker chord for a stronger, lightening the cadence. He might have felt it was wise to do so, it gets repeated so many times.

After awhile a small chorus in the pit joins in and sings the three bass notes on the syllables La, Sol, and Do. These syllables are part of the Italian *solfeggio* system used for sight singing. Do, Re, Mi, Fa, Sol, La, Ti, Do indicate the notes of any diatonic scale. Instead of a text, the singers are simply telling you the names of the notes as they sing them. Then they begin counting the durations of the notes—one, two, three, four, and so forth. (Einstein: mathematics, get it?) They're singing the rhythm. It's wonderful. You don't have the burden of a text about Einstein or anything else, for that matter. Someone once asked Philip what *Einstein* meant. He replied that it didn't mean anything, it simply was what it was. However one cannot forget that Einstein's formula, $e = mc^2$, made the atomic bomb possible, and that Stanley Kubrick's movie *On the Beach* depicted the world after a nuclear holocaust. There is a long trial scene in the opera, too.

When we try to explain the theory of relativity, we can use as an example throwing a ball up in the air inside a moving train. The ball is moving vertically while the train is moving horizontally. Time and space are relative. That perhaps accounts for the image of a train in *Einstein*. Or maybe Wilson simply wanted to have a train on stage. Anyway, a huge locomotive moves on stage imperceptibly slowly until it's totally in view, then there's a blackout and it's gone. It reappears several times. This wouldn't happen in the movies or traditional opera. Repeating it gives you another chance to see it. Someone asked Bob why his works were so repetitive and slow. He answered that he wanted the audience to have time to think about them.

Let's pretend we're on an anthropological mission to another planet. We come upon what looks like a written formula or graffiti of some kind. After a little study, we discover that it is shorthand for a musical harmonic phrase, indicating a modulation (change) from one key to another. Here's what it looks like:

f------D♭-------B♭♭
(i) (vi) (ivb)
A-----B-----E
(IV) (V) (I)

Small letters indicate minor chords; capitals, major ones. B♭♭ (B double flat) is the same chord as A spelled enharmonically. This chord acts as a pivot between the keys of *f minor* and *E major*. Philip repeats this harmonic progression over and over again, each time varying the durations of each chord. It sounds like an object being looked at from various angles or in changing light conditions. In traditional music this progression would have been used to get from one place to another. In *Einstein* it goes nowhere.

Satyagraha

At the end of Philip Glass's opera *Satyagraha* (1980) Mahatma Gandhi sings one of the most poignant arias in all opera. It is in Sanskrit and consists of thirty repetitions—ten groups of three—of the same upward Phrygian modal scale. The Phrygian mode is one of the so-called medieval church modes that were thought to be recreations of the ancient Greek modes.

Each mode is characterized by a particular pattern of whole and half steps around a central tone (tonic). If you start a scale on each of the notes of a diatonic scale on the white keys on the piano, for example, you have the patterns of the medieval church modes. If you randomly let your fingers wander over these white keys, beginning and ending on each mode's *final* (beginning and ending tone) you hear its distinct personality. We have lost the subtlety of hearing the rich emotions connected with these modes in favor of the more generic sounds of the major and minor keys. In ancient

Greece one mode was outlawed because it was thought that it promoted lascivious conduct. Imagine that! That's what they used to say about jazz; that's what they say about rock and roll now. That's why we like these musics so much.

Starting from the note E on the piano keyboard and playing the white notes upward to the E an octave above will automatically generate the Phrygian mode. The melodic results of even random choices of these notes will sound unmistakably Phrygian and produce an emotional effect distinctive of that mode. As you move up the keyboard you will discover that the interval pattern of whole and half steps is as follows: half, whole, whole, whole, half, whole (E, F, G, A, B, C, D, E). There's a semitone (half step) at the beginning, a whole tone at the top. The pattern of a major scale, on the other hand, is whole, whole, half, whole, whole, whole, half. It has a whole step at the bottom, a half step at the top. This half step is called a leading tone. A leading tone gives a strong unambiguous push to the tonic, or final tone of the scale. It is partly responsible for the assertiveness of Western music. The leading tone is contained in the dominant (V) chord which, when followed by the tonic (I), is the strongest chord progression in Western classical harmony.

By having Gandhi sing a Phrygian scale over and over again, Glass emphasizes the non-violent aspect of Gandhi's political philosophy. The half step at the beginning (E-F) gives a push up to the tone above it, a sort of leading tone to the second degree of the scale. The whole step at the top (D-E) produces a softer cadence. The combination of half step at the beginning and whole step at the top gives this simple scalar structure a feeling of upward expansion. It reminds me of thirty flowers blossoming, one after the other. If you invert the Phrygian scale—EDCBAGFE—it becomes sort of an upside down major scale. It's as if Gandhi were turning Western culture on its head.

Perfect Lives

Sometime around 1970 or so, the Sonic Arts Union was performing at Antioch College in Yellow Springs, Ohio. After the concert, Bob and I went out for a drink. Since Yellow Springs was dry, we had to drive to Xenia (coincidentally, the name of John Cage's first wife), Ohio. We drove through cornfields. You know how straight those roads are. Pretty soon we came upon a roadhouse. We went in and the first thing we saw was a huge electric organ. It was just sitting there idle. I think it was a Wurlitzer. There was a row of men and women sitting up at the bar talking to each other very seriously. It seemed to me that none of the couples was married because they were having such interesting conversations. They were having fun, smoking and drinking. We sat down and Bob started talking about Jimmy Smith, the jazz organist, and the legendary pianist Bud Powell. After awhile we went into Xenia to get something to eat. When we stopped at the same roadhouse on our way back, the scene was exactly the same. Here were these lives going on and on. It felt timeless.

Since the early Eighties, Robert Ashley has made a series of operas to be shown on television. The first one he made was called *Perfect Lives* (1978–1980), subtitled *Private Parts*. The work consists of seven episodes. Each one is twenty-five minutes and so many seconds, the length of time of a half-hour TV program, including announcements. I would be hard put to explain what the opera is about, except that the Mid-Western American landscape plays an important role. The locales for each scene—*The Bank*, *The Bar*, *The Church*, *The Backyard*, *The Living Room*—are places that people go practically every day. There's no reason you couldn't write an opera about them. The action doesn't take place in a palace or on a battlefield. *Perfect Lives* is about everyday American life.

When landscape is the idea you don't have to worry about the story. You don't have to worry about a narrative because a landscape exists by itself and says so much. Shifting visual images. A landscape has no intended story. In writing about this work in an essay called "And So It Goes Depending" Bob says, "I was only typing what I had rehearsed again and again in speech . . . I discovered that I could sort out in the piles of typed paragraphs, those that had come from different rhythmic sources, and by that I mean paragraphs of repetitions of certain simple phrases and a variety of different word combinations. Some of which made sense, and others not so much." Robert Rauschenberg told me once that as a child he had difficulty reading and writing. He would look at a page and see only the patterns of all the A's, for example. If you read a page of text and you see visual patterns instead of meanings on the page, then you must be dyslexic. We think of it as a sort of sickness. Ashley finds rhymes as he's reading prose.

Elsewhere Bob says he has lost his taste for mechanical amplification, including the piano whose sounds are amplified by a soundboard. He says his taste is to want every sound to be electronically amplified:

> I've lost my taste for the tempo of mechanical life. In it's representation in, say, vocal projection. I like sounds that formally were too soft or too short or too quick. In any tradition, those sounds to the degree that they are recognized are called nuance. They are recognized as attachments to the main form. Wonderful violinists have a sense of nuance, or the nuances are the smaller details or the small inflections on something. They do the smallest possible things that one can to make a string sound wonderfully. Now we are all in blizzard of nuance, so dense that the main form is lost.

Perhaps Bob means that we concentrate on everything that's incidental, that's not really essential. That's something to think about. He also goes so far as to state, "I think on New Years Eve, I'll sit like many other people in the world and watch it on television. And not go out in the world, but watch the world on television."

He also talks about how essential collaboration is. For example, the piano playing in *Perfect Lives* is by Blue "Gene" Tyranny (the tyranny of one's genes). There was a beautiful Hollywood actress in the Forties named Gene Tierney (*Leave Her to Heaven, 1945*). Imagine writing an opera and leaving the music up to someone else! What an extreme idea! Bob worked for years with the ONCE Group in Ann Arbor, Michigan. He was sort of the father figure and even if he didn't generate all the ideas, nobody would have gotten them if he hadn't been there. Everyone wanted to think creatively when in his presence.

Dust

Robert Ashley has composed over twenty-six operas over a span of thirty years. He originally planned them as operas for television but so far only one has actually appeared on television. They are so different that TV producers won't touch them. But no matter, really, because they sound wonderful simply presented in concert as oratorios. Webster's Dictionary defines an oratorio as a lengthy choral work usually of a religious nature consisting chiefly of recitatives, arias, and choruses without action or scenery. This might describe Ashley's operas but without the religiosity. In *Celestial Excursions*, for example, the performers simply sit at tables facing the audience. In *Dust* they stand behind opaque plasma screens. And in *The Making of Concrete* they step out in front of a table to tell their stories reading from what look like oversize playing cards. The simplicity of these presentations makes it easy for the viewer to listen to the music without the distraction of histrionics.

Virtually all Bob's operas have employed the same five performers: singers Jackie Humbert, Joan La Barbara, Sam Ashley, Tom Buckner, and sound engineer Tom Hamilton. They remind me of the Duke Ellington Band that included among others Harry

Carney, Barney Bigard, and Johnny Hodges, who made Ellington's sound so strange and beautiful.

Opera as we know it has traditionally consisted chiefly of recitatives, arias, choruses, and orchestral interludes. *Grove's Dictionary of Music* defines recitative as "a type of vocal writing, normally for a single voice, which follows closely the natural rhythm and accentuation of speech, without necessarily being governed by a regular tempo or organized in a specific form." The *Harvard Dictionary of Music* says, "Recitative is a vocal style designed to imitate and emphasize the natural inflections of human speech."

Recitative has been present in opera since Monteverdi's great *Orfeo* of 1607. Then it went into decline. In Gluck's *Orfeo ed Eurydice* of 1762 it became conventional, simply moving the action forward between arias. Gluck did, however, perfect the aria form, creating utterly simple although asymmetrical song-like pieces. Stravinsky, in his *Rake's Progress* of 1954 resurrected the dry (sec) recitative with solo harpsichord cadential punctuations, a blatant reference to Mozart in whose operas recitatives are much like patter songs.

Arias are solos that exist out of time. Often they are still moments where the action stops and something musical happens, not in an active sense but how the singer feels at that moment. In Monteverdi's *Orfeo* (1607) there are no true arias, only places where arias would be appropriate. What propels the work along to an unparalleled degree are the recitatives. The words dominate the music, the melodic lines follow and are generated by the words. Ashley's vocal style, with its emphasis on speech, closely resembles Monteverdi's recitative style. In fact we could consider it an advance on Monteverdi.

In *Dust* the characters are homeless people who inhabit a small park outside Ashley's downtown New York loft. Each of them tells a story, sad and funny at the same time. In most of his operas the characters are ordinary folks, not celebrities as in many recent operas, for example, Einstein, Nixon, or Gandhi. Bob insists that everybody has a story worth telling. He said that, when he came to New York from California, he was fascinated by the ranting and raving of those disturbed people who roam the streets of New York. He said that he "studied" ranting as he walked the streets and learned a lot about speech singing from them.

Typically, Bob assigns the singers specific pitches that they extract from given sounding material through headphones or stage monitor loudspeakers. In *Foreign Experiences*, for example, Jackie Humbert is asked to extract the note A-flat from a chord positioned down the right side of the score page. You can see what it looks like in the accompanying illustration.

This chord could be found in any dance band arrangement. However Bob lets the singers alter those pitches to bring out the stress and accents of the words. He discovered an elegant way of producing different vocal characters within a single voice. By giving the singer a high pitch, a certain vocal character is produced; a lower one produces a different character. He may have gotten the idea from Ray Charles, whom Bob greatly admired and who changed his vocal persona to wonderful effect.

The Making of Concrete

The Making of Concrete (2007) consists of intimate stories about four of Bob's close friends from his past. The stories are about illegal activities, including drug dealing and cheating at poker. One of the stories even relates Bob's efforts at the seduction of the girlfriend of one of his closest friends. It's sort of a *True Confessions*. Rather than notating pitches for the singers they take their pitches freely from a dense electronic sound accompaniment that surrounds them. This accompaniment consists of thousands of sound samples that Bob had designed and mixed and spatialized by Tom Hamilton. Hamilton calls himself an "invisible performer."

Foreign Experiences: Act I - The Flying Serpent Page 6

4 beats per line @ 90 beats/minute

				Sam Chorus	Jackie Amy	Joan Margh.	Tom Bob
Jackie	121	It's on the far other end of the building	IIIb		A♭		
	122	Also I don't know what floor it's on					
	123	Ten years and I don't know what floor it's on					
	124	Where I keep stuff I work with so as					
Sam & Jackie	125	To unclutter the studio to make room		C	A♭		
	126	For people who don't have an office					
CAPTION	127	Between studio and Office there are two ways ∠ to get there		C	A♭	G	E♮
	128	At, say, three in the morning one way is down outside					
	129	Across and up that's a long walk at, say,	IIIa	E♭	C	B♭	F
	130	Three in the morning the other is straight through the building					
	131	Straight through the back of the Concert Hall across the					
	132	Very back row hope the Exit sign is working					
Marghreta*	133	This night in question I made four trips				B♭	
	134	Each one a little more weird than the last					
	135	Full grown man each more weird than the last				B♭	F
Marg & Tom	136	∠ Finally ∠ I can't do it ∠					
	137	∠ I have to admit I'm afraid ∠					
	138	∠ I am afraid to go through there ∠					
Tom & Amy	139	∠ That's the only way I can say it ∠			C		F
	140	∠ I am afraid to go through there ∠					
Amy & Joan	141	Not afraid of the dark ∠ ∠			C	B♭	
	142	Not afraid of the silence ∠ ∠					
	143	Just afraid ∠ ∠ ∠					
	144	End of scene four El Dorado scene five					

Page 6 of Robert Ashley's Foreign Experiences, *1994.*
Used by permission of the composer.

Skin, Meat, Bone

In 1994 Anthony Braxton asked me to do a festival of my music at Wesleyan. I didn't want to do it. I thought it was too egotistic to do a festival of one's own work at one's own school. Anthony, who was Chair of the Music Department at the time, insisted. Someone suggested I simply do two concerts, one on a Friday night, another on Saturday, and that's it. I decided against it. I decided that it would be one week long and without the academic stuff—no panel discussions, no papers, just concerts and installations.

A few years before, I had flown into New York from Europe and immediately went to the Brooklyn Academy of Music to see *Black Rider* by Robert Wilson. I was jet lagged and almost fell asleep up in the balcony. I started dreaming about how much I would love to collaborate with Wilson on a theater work. That's like saying I want to be in a movie with Christopher Plummer. So when I began thinking about what to do I thought about collaborating with artists I admired. I asked Sol LeWitt to supply a wall drawing for the Zilhka Gallery and invited John Ashbery, whom I had met in Germany a couple of years before, to do a reading on the Poetry Series. I wrote to Bob Wilson, whom I had met a few times, but somebody told me he never reads his mail. He collects all of his faxes and has somebody read them to him. He can't be bothered, he's so busy. Finally, I called Ronald Vance, an old friend of mine from college who worked for Bob, and asked his advice. He told me to come to an installation Bob was mounting the following week in Soho. I showed up and Ronald introduced me to him. Bob said that he would love to make something for Wesleyan and that I should make plans to visit him at his summer workshop in Watermill, Long Island, the following summer. Every summer Bob develops pieces at Watermill. Students from all over the world come to work on theater productions. We arranged for me to come to Watermill in late August. In the meantime he told me to get in touch with Keith McDermott, an actor with whom he often worked.

I filled my car up in with materials, including a motor-driven door I could steer with a remote control model sailboat steering device. It would zigzag across the space slowly. As it did so, it would reflect and move across the space a high pitched sound wave beamed at it. I thought Bob would like that, it would give him something to see. I also brought a digital delay system that could recycle sounds in real time. I thought that actors could do a live version of *I Am Sitting in a Room* somewhere in the course of the work. I also brought a glass tube and a Bunsen burner. When a flame is inserted in the tube, it excites the tube at its resonant frequency, making a beautiful sound. I thought it would look beautiful on stage. Bob is a genius with props and objects on stage. In *Orlando*, a little gold box suddenly appears on the floor from nowhere. He collects props from all over the world. He has a collection of over a hundred chairs stored at Watermill, including a regal throne he designed for a production of *King Lear*. As we rehearsed Bob would ask for certain props as he went along: a certain fabric, a circular paper hat, a roll of paper towel, a three-pronged wooden rake. He was thinking geometrically, I think; the hat was a circle, the rake a trident, the paper towel a cylinder, and so on. Anyway, I showed Bob all my things.

The next morning he asked for seven apprentice actors. They came into his studio and sat on the floor. One by one he asked them to get up and begin slowly walking across the floor. He added actors one by one, asking them to maintain the body positions—hands on hips, arms folded etc.—they had when seated, and proceeded to choreograph them walking forward and back across the room in beautiful patterns. As I sat watching I asked Bob to stop for a moment while I tuned a pure wave oscillator to middle D, a tone all of them could hum. I instructed the actors to hum only when they were moving. Because the pitch of their humming could not exactly match the oscillator tone, audible beating—bumps of sound as the waves collide—could be clearly heard.

During another scene I noticed an actor walking slowly across the back of the stage and asked Bob if we could stop while I got a snare drum for the actor to carry with him. The drum would resonate only when it moved through crests of oscillator-generated sound waves flowing from a pair of loudspeakers. I would interrupt Bob as I got ideas and without hesitation he would stop his work to let this happen. He never suggested changes. Everything I proposed flowed smoothly into the piece. Bob outlined nine scenes: three portraits (close-ups); three still lives (medium shots); three landscapes (long shots). The form was ABC, ABC, ABC. Bob choreographed a scene a day for nine days. I supplied sound for each scene. What a thrill.

The actors wore white tee shirts with no pockets, pressed tan khaki pants and sneakers. No jewelry, watches or earrings. Keith McDermott had come to campus a few weeks earlier to audition the student actors. He had them walk across the stage taking two minutes to do so. He worked hard on their posture, telling them to imagine they could see behind them, to think of the space behind them. Some of these students had never been on the stage before, they just came in and auditioned. They looked like statues that stepped off the Parthenon frieze. Look at that lighting! Up in back there's a white scrim. Bob wanted a white scrim from ceiling to floor with not a single wrinkle in it.

Bob doesn't start with a libretto or text or plot. He is totally visual. As he talks with you he is constantly drawing on a piece of paper. His theater works are spectacles and could be wordless. Any text he uses is simply layered on or placed into the action in some way. The texts we used in this work are taken from *I Remember*, a book by Joe Brainard, that simply consists of short sentences that begin with the phrase "I remember." You finish the sentence with a memory, something simple and unpretentious. It has been used in teaching young children to get started writing. We let the students invent their own sentences. In one scene they were recycled through the space as in *I Am Sitting in a Room*. Here are a couple of examples:

> "I remember going to the park with my mother."
> "I remember getting chewing gum stuck in my hair."
> "I remember my brother putting his pants on backwards."

In one scene a couple of actors took turns waving around a video camera. They simply picked it up in one hand and swung it wherever their arms moved so the images are totally random. In another I put sounds of whispering through the delay system using shorter delays than in the *I Remember* section. Three of the actors wore lavaliere microphones, enough to pick up everybody's sounds. Bob had to persuade the actors not to look sad, just to whisper, that's all. There wasn't any reason to show emotion. In one scene he added a few giggles. I didn't particularly like the giggling, but it gives a mysterious quality to the work. In another scene the actors carried sticks that made beautiful sounds when they softly hit each other. In the second portrait I put closely tuned pure sound waves in citronella pails hoping that the audience could hear the sounds beating against one another. In another an actor washes his feet. Throughout the work various actors would do little mysterious activities like that. Bob sees the motions simply as visual, such as bringing a pail down on one's head. He doesn't intend it to mean anything in particular and yet there is meaning in it. Each audience member supplies meaning for him or herself. For one of the still lives I found three small resonant objects: a milk bottle, a conch shell, and a purple vase I picked up at a tag sale a couple of hours before the performance. Originally we were going to use a hollow ostrich egg but during rehearsal a stagehand dropped it and it shattered. The actors inserted miniature microphones in them. As they recited their *I Remember* sentences into the objects the resonances modulated the speech.

When Bob was constructing the last landscape at Watermill a sudden windstorm came up. He ran to the window and saw trees swaying and being blown by the wind. He asked a couple of assistants go outside and collect armfuls of dead and live limbs. Then he asked for a sheaf of wheat. In the final landscape first the actors bring the dead limbs in, then they run off and bring in the green ones, waving them as they do so. The trees have such a beautiful presence on stage. One actor runs in circles carrying the sheaf of wheat. The moving door appears in the last scene, too. It moves very slowly migrating across the stage beaming the high sound across the audience. It was controlled with a remote control device, by a student in the balcony.

Skin, Meat, Bone was presented at Wesleyan in 1994 with fourteen student actors. As Bob was sketching out the work, he said: "You know, I think of it as the skin, meat and bone of my work." When the time came to give the work a title, I sent him a fax suggesting *Skin, Meat, Bone*. He answered: "How about *Skin, Meat, Bone: The Wesleyan Project*"? I said okay.

18

WORDS

Empty Words

When John Cage came to Wesleyan in the early Seventies, he carried with him the journals of Thoreau. He said he found wonderful things on every page, not to mention phrases concerned with sound. He said that Thoreau thought about sounds the way electronic musicians thought about them. Thoreau described the sounds of telegraph wires he heard for the first time. Concord, Massachusetts, 1851. Thoreau would hear the wires singing. They were Aeolian harps. Imagine hearing telegraph wires humming for the first time! Thoreau was excited about the sounds of nature and about the new sounds. Anyway, in *Empty Words* (1973–1978) Cage subjected the texts of Thoreau to chance operations on five levels: letters, syllables, words, phrases, and sentences. There were twenty-five combinations of these so he simply related the number sixty-four to the number twenty-five. He used the *I Ching* to choose pages and lines of the text as well as random combinations of the components listed above. Then he worked them together to make a text, which he would then recite in a half chant or dramatic sound-inflected style. It sounded like an ancient soothsayer or shaman chanting.

The text is in four parts. The first consists of combinations of letters, syllables, words, and phrases. The second part consists of letters, syllables, and words. The third, only letters and syllables, and by the fourth part, there is nothing left but individual letters and silences. For all-night performances, the windows would be opened at dawn to let in the outside sounds.

Cage performed part of *Empty Words* in Crowell Hall in the early Seventies. He came to this class and threw the *I Ching* to generate a score for altering the volume, balance, bass, and treble controls on an amplifier. At twenty-seven seconds, for example, the treble control is rotated to three o'clock, increasing the high frequencies. Then the bass is boosted. Simple manipulations such as these give the performance an electronic quality. The chance operations serve to interdict the syntax, destroy the meaning, and turn speech into music. Cage isn't making speech superhuman; he's not elevating the human voice the way you find in opera, making it grander and more serious than it really is. By simply rearranging everyday speech he makes it musical. He's showing how we are connected to the technological world, too.

In Sara, Mencken Christ and Beethoven There Were Men and Women

What a beautiful title! Sara is writer Sara Powell Haardt, writer and spouse of H. L. Mencken, American journalist and critic. We all know who Christ is and, of course, Beethoven. This poem is by John Barton Wolgamot, an obscure figure who worked as manager of the Little Carnegie Cinema in New York. The poem, written in 1944, was discovered by poet and publisher (Burning Deck) Keith Waldrop as he was browsing through a used bookstore. He showed it to Bob Ashley who immediately took a liking to it, so much that he decided to make a large vocal work out of its text. It is a litany of famous people.

In Sara, Mencken (1972) consists of a hundred and twenty-eight stanzas, each one a single run-on sentence occupying its own page. Here is the first one:

> In its very truly great manners of Ludwig van Beethoven very heroically the very cruelly ancestral death of Sarah Powell Haardt had very ironically come amongst his very really grand men and

> women to Rafael Sabatini, George Ade, Margaret Strom Jameson, Ford Madox Hueffer, Jean-Jacques Bernard, Louis Bromfield, Friedrich Wilhelm Nietzche, and Helen Brown Norden very titanically.

The stanzas are virtually of the same construction with the exception of four variables, including names and adverbs. Bob looked at this and saw that there were no stopping points or punctuation marks along the way to give the reader pause, except for commas separating the names. Realizing this he decided to read each stanza in one breath. He recorded all of them, then spliced out the spaces between them producing one entire uninterrupted reading. This gives the listener little or no time to breathe creating a somewhat uneasy feeling. Along with composer Paul DeMarinis, Bob devised seven configurations of Moog synthesizer modules, filters actually, that analyze seven components of his voice, including fundamental frequencies, plosive attacks, and harmonics. As the vocal sounds flow through the components they trigger electronic sounds creating a rich and varied tapestry of sound. Ashley's voice creates the accompaniment. The recording is about forty minutes long.

Americans love lists. The Lewis and Clark expedition went out West and listed all the flowers. In *In Sara, Mencken*, there is a litany of names. Fourteen of them — seven men and seven women — reappear often, numerous others are repeated several times and hundreds of others occur only once, creating a sort of hierarchy of names that suggests a certain form not readily discernable to the listener. Nonetheless, they acquire a kind of beautiful grandeur.

Automatic Writing

Automatic writing was a technique used by the surrealists to generate images that didn't come from their rational consciousness. You can see why John Cage was interested in the surrealists. I met Cage once a couple of years ago in Germany, before he died. He had been sick and had gone to a German doctor, who ran a magnet over his body to make his diagnosis. And John said, "Oh, it was wonderful. He didn't have to use his intelligence!" Anyway, the idea is that there's intelligence that comes from various sources, in one case magnetism, and in another automatic writing. In the Forties, John Cage, Virgil Thomson, Lou Harrison, and others wrote pieces in which each one would write a section. They would agree on such things as meter and length but otherwise wouldn't know what the others were writing. They called it *Exquisite Corpse*, after a parlor game used by the surrealists in 1925.

In some of my composition classes, the first thing I do when I see that student composers are stuck for ideas is to suggest that they try automatic writing. I may give them thirty seconds to think about it, then write down what immediately comes to mind. It's a way to get unstuck when you can't work. It can give you beautiful and unexpected results.

In the Seventies many people were envious of my speech impediment—I stutter. (See the last sentence of "*I Am Sitting in a Room*.") People would come up to me and explain that although one couldn't tell from hearing them talk, in fact they stuttered. I never believed them and was amused by their desire to suffer the embarrassment that comes with stuttering. Anyway, Bob Ashley used to tell me that secretly he stuttered. I told him that I really didn't believe that he did. A few years later he came up with the notion that he had Tourette's Syndrome.

In the liner notes to the recording of *Automatic Writing* (1979), Bob states that he thinks he has a touch of Tourette's. It is an imaginative way of explaining involuntary speech, which is the basic sound source of the recording of *Automatic Writing*. These involuntary utterances, processed by a switching circuit designed by Paul DeMarinis, as well as intermittent whispers in French, some mysterious organ music, and ambient sounds as if heard through the walls of an apartment next door, make up the sound material of the piece.

Recently mezzo soprano Priscilla Dunstan presented the idea that there are universal sound reflexes in babies from birth to three months old. For example, "Neh" means "I'm hungry"; "Owh" means "I'm sleepy." If she is correct (her theory is yet to be proven) then what we thought of as simply random grunts and gurgles may now be considered as involuntary signals common to all human infants. We could, I suppose, analyze Bob's utterances as having meaning, to him at least, if not to everyone. One could indicate anguish, sadness, regret.

In those days many people distrusted language or at least grammar. William Burroughs once said, "Language is a virus from outer space." N. O. Brown said somewhere that when he hears grammar he thinks of an army marching.

Love Is a Good Example

I remember touring with Bob Ashley in the Midwest. At parties after concerts we would often stand around listening to people speaking. If he listened attentively, he could hear the singsongy inflections in ordinary folks' speech. The more one listens to everyday speech the more it sounds like melody. Simple phrases such as "Are you going to the movies tonight?" "Well, I don't know, I guess so," are inherently musical. There are wonderful melodies in everyday speech. "Love is a good example" is a musical phrase by itself but it becomes more so because of the way Bob accentuates certain words and resonances.

There's a fine line between speech and song. When did human beings begin singing? Chant is simply sustaining a pitch, or two or three pitches, and reciting a text before it gets more florid and melismatic (several notes sung on one syllable). *Love Is a Good Example* (1987) is an unaccompanied vocal solo that exhibits a very different way of thinking about words, song, and speech. I find myself having a problem figuring out where it lies. What name do I give it? Do I call it music? Do I call it song? Do I call it some sort of exaggerated speech? Then I think what a ridiculous task I've put on myself that I've got to give it a label. The more I listen to it the more it sounds like music. Its form even resembles a rondo; the refrain, "Love, sure, is a good example," comes back and back again—twenty-six times, in fact. Think of refrains in poetry and music. But each time the word "sure" is repeated Bob says it in a different way to give it a different meaning. It may sound optimistic or sarcastic depending on how Bob enunciates it.

The words are in columns, and he indicates a metronome marking of 72 beats per minute. Each grouping is in a three-beat rhythm and follows it more or less accurately. The "sti" in the word "statistics" is a grace note.

She Was a Visitor

She Was a Visitor by Bob Ashley is a choral work. The title refers to a young woman we knew who died by her own hand. John Cage has a story about a suicide. A young child kills himself. A Buddhist monk was asked, "Why would he do such a thing?" The monk answered that perhaps he was correcting an error. I don't know what I think about that story. "She was a visitor" is a more beautiful way of saying it.

Throughout the course of the piece a speaker repeats the phrase, "She was a visitor." Bob notates the phrase in $\frac{3}{4}$ time. "She was a" and "visitor" are notated in triplets. Triplets are when you squash three notes into the time it takes for two notes to sound. Bob embeds two sets of three in a rhythmic pattern of three. The chorus is split into any number of groups each having a leader. From time to time the leaders choose a phoneme as the main speaker is pronouncing it. Say you decide on "sh" from "she." You wait for the speaker to utter "sh" from the word "She," then you sustain the sound for one breath. As you do so the rest of the group picks up that phoneme—they don't know in advance what it is going to be—and sustain it for one breath also. Because reaction times vary the sounds spread out through the groups. It's a way of taking apart an English phrase and isolating the phonemes in it, making choral music. There's no "s" sound in the piece. There's only "sh," "ih," "oo," "ah," "zz," "uh," "v," "ih," "zz," "ih," "t," and "er." It isn't pronounced "visit-or." Bob is from the Midwest. He pronounces it "visiter."

Different Trains

The title *Different Trains* (1988) refers to the trains that took Jewish people to Auschwitz and other death camps during World War II versus the trains that, as a young boy, Steve Reich used to take from New York to Los Angeles, to visit one of his divorced parents. To depict the rhythm of the wheels of the trains he used the *paradiddle*, a basic drum pattern that all drummers practice to acquire right and left hand equality. The alternation of the right and left hands follows this pattern: RLRRLRLL. Try playing this yourself and see how difficult it is to keep both hands rhythmically even. For melodic material Steve recorded various voices, including a retired Pullman porter crying out departure times for these fast trains, for example, "New York to Chicago" and "Chicago to Los Angeles," in addition to fragments of interviews with Holocaust survivors. He listened carefully to the inflections of these recordings, then wrote them down in musical notation for the string players. During a performance you can hear the recorded voices as well as their instrumental counterparts.

Throughout the piece you hear the wailing of train whistles, too. When Steve came to Wesleyan in the late Eighties for a performance of his *Octet*, he showed a group of graduate composers how, by routing the sounds through a Casio sampler and using the keyboard, he could change the pitch of any train whistle to fit the harmony of the string music. Even though the piece was written for the four players of the Kronos Quartet, Steve instructs the players to overdub parts of the music three times forming a sixteen-voice texture.

This is not the first time that everyday speech has been used in music. The Czech composer Leoš Janáček (1854–1928) used to jot down in a notebook fragments of speech he overheard on the streets of his hometown, Brno. He was interested in the pitch curves and rhythms, paying attention to the moods of the speakers. He would then notate them and use them as material for his operas.

19
VOICES

Three Voices

It just started snowing outside so let's listen to *Three Voices* by Morton Feldman. It was written for Joan La Barbara. Her voice is pre-recorded on two channels of tape. She's the third voice. Joan stands between two loudspeakers. Feldman thought of the speakers as tombstones or cenotaphs for his friends Philip Guston and Frank O'Hara, who had died a couple years earlier. Although the music is continuous, it is in distinct sections: opening, legato (smooth), slow waltz, first words, whisper, snowfall, and so forth.

The form has a proportion you would never expect: the text doesn't come in until about ten minutes after the beginning. Feldman uses only one line of the poem, "Who'd have thought / that snow falls," from *Wind*, which was written for him by Frank O'Hara.

Feldman uses only the first line of the poem. Why? Perhaps because he's not primarily interested in setting a text. He's more interested in the sound of Joan's voice. All he needs is one line. This singing style has no vibrato. Vibrato is when you make your voice shake a little bit to give it warmth. String players use vibrato to get a warm tone. It was a nineteenth-century idea, to enhance the sound. We don't use vibrato much anymore. We want the sound to be pure and clean.

One of the characteristics of long oral works is that the same adjectives occur over and over again. In *The Odyssey* the sea is always "wine-dark" or "wine-blue." You can't expect the poet to think up new adjectives for the same noun. You need repetition. In Feldman's long works, motives repeat with little differences. Italo Calvino was criticized for including several versions of the same story in his edition of *Italian Folk Tales*. Each village tells the same tale with little details changed. Feldman had a large collection of Turkish rugs. He loved the patterns in them that repeat with minute differences.

Turtle Dreams

When Meredith Monk was young she studied the Dalcroze Method of *Eurhythmics*. Jacques Dalcroze was a Swiss musician and music educator who developed a method of learning and experiencing music through movement. When I was at Yale in the Fifties I remember that harpsichordist Ralph Kirkpatrick would make his students walk the tempos and rhythms of the pieces they were studying to better get the feel of the music. He also made them sing one of the contrapuntal lines of a Bach two-part invention while playing the second one. This helped keyboard players become more musical, to connect their physical bodies to the music they were playing. Meredith, however, says that she was uncoordinated as a child and used singing to help her move better. In *Turtle Dreams* (1982) four performers move in shifting patterns while singing repetitive phrases. They don't move to the music, they move with the music.

I first heard Meredith sing at a Merce Cunningham event in the early Seventies. I thought I was listening to all the women in the world singing with one voice. There were no words, only syllables and phonemes that sounded as if they came from real or imaginary cultures. Since the beginning Meredith's output has been almost entirely vocal. In certain songs she overdubs her voice but confesses that she would rather use two human singers. In a couple of duets from *Volcano Songs* (1993) she makes two voices — her own and Katie Geissinger's — sound like one. These two singers are so rhythmically in sync and have such similar intonation that they sound like one person singing. It's uncanny. On the other hand, in such pieces as *Click Song No. 1* from *Light Songs* (1988) she turns one voice into two by making simultaneous clicking noises that sound as if they are being made by a second performer. They remind me of the click languages of the Bushmen of southern Africa. There is a lovely irony in these songs: two voices sound like one; one sounds like two. In 1976 Meredith took some time off from New York, went out west to Santa Fe where she spent a couple of months all by herself. She sat on a hill and composed *Songs from the Hill*.

Meredith Monk is a true intermedia artist. We might define intermedia as a mixture of two or more art forms that interpenetrate each other, superimposing principles from one art form upon another. For example, I remember in *Education of the Girlchild* (1972) there is one scene in which a woman sets a teacup down upon a table. She repeats this action several times. That would never happen in a play or in a movie. Repetition does happen in music, however, and in some writing, particularly that of Gertrude Stein. Meredith is superimposing a musical structure onto a theatrical action. As you watch the same physical action over and over again you discover small differences, things about it you would have missed if you only saw it once. You get a more complete picture of the action. Mixed media or multimedia simply means mixing two or more art forms in one composition. The surrealist ballet *Parade* (1917), a collaboration between Erik Satie, Pablo Picasso, and Jean Cocteau, with choreography by Leonide Massine, is a good example of a mixed media work. Satie imagined an orchestra of noisemakers. (There was a typewriter in the percussion section.) Picasso designed cubist sculptures out of cardboard, making it difficult for the dancers to move. It was similar to most stage works in which you have music and action, each supporting the other. The adventurous and radical spirit of *Parade* must have inspired

Merce Cunningham and John Cage, except that in their collaborations the composers and artists worked wholly independently without having seen the dance. In fact, in many instances the dancers hadn't heard the music until opening night.

Hay Una Mujer Desaparecida

Christian Wolff made a series of political pieces that caused him to have a sharp difference of opinion with John Cage. Cage felt that you should not fight fire with fire, and that political music was as bad as politics. If you're anti-fascist and you write a socialistic music, it takes on the same attributes as the fascist music. It becomes assertive and militant. Susan Sontag once said that communism *was* fascism. Cage felt he was being revolutionary by making works that were inherently different from the works that had grown up in the Western capitalistic society and that he was being political in that way.

Christian elected to be political in a local way. He used union songs and wrote pieces that evoked the slogans of Mao. In the 1970s in Chile, the fascist government was abducting people from their homes at night; many were never seen again. In 1979 Christian wrote a set of variations on singer Holly Near's song, *Hay una Mujer Desaparecida* (*There is a Woman Missing*), a lament for the women who "disappeared" under Pinochet's regime in Chile.

Theme and variation is a classical music form in which a composer takes a simple melody and writes variations on it. Mozart used *Twinkle, Twinkle, Little Star*, for example, as the basis for a set of twelve variations (K.265/300e). J. S. Bach's *Goldberg Variations* is a set of thirty-two variations written on a simple binary-form piece. Bach uses ornamentation, changes of meter, rhythm, and harmony, canons at various intervals, virtually every technique in his repertoire.

Hay una Mujer Desaparecida is completely written out. Christian said that when he started writing works for musical instruments, using pitches, not sounds, he decided to notate them precisely. He also wanted his music to be more conventional in order to appeal to a wider audience. But even he admits that the music is quirkier than ever. Since the coordinations and cueing of his early works lead to unexpected juxtapositions and correlations, Christian's fully notated pieces follow the same quirkiness and illogical sequences. One thing doesn't flow to the next in any logical order. Events happen one after the other in much the same way they do in his coordination pieces.

As composers become political, their music becomes less experimental. The focus is on the political idea not the intrinsic or aesthetic value of the music itself. The music is about something else, something outside the aesthetic domain. There are those who question the aesthetic domain entirely, who say that all music is political, and that, even if you're not political, you're upholding the status quo.

20

STRING QUARTETS

The Grosse Fuge

When I was a student at Tanglewood in the late Fifties, I met the South American composer Mario Davidovsky, who was a student there also. We were having coffee one morning, and I asked him about his music. Because his English at that time was poor, he took out his music-writing pen and drew a long arc over the nineteenth century. He wrote Beethoven's name on one side, Schoenberg's on the other. He said, "For me the history of music goes all the way over the nineteenth century to Schoenberg." There was nothing in between.

The twentieth-century string quartet starts with Beethoven's *Grosse Fuge*, Opus 133, written in 1825 and published as a separate work in 1827. It was originally the final movement of Beethoven's quartet, Op. 130, but it was such a tour de force that Beethoven decided it should stand by itself. Beethoven wrote it toward the end of his life. He died in 1827. So this is one of his imaginings, one of his fantasies, as an old man who was deaf already, and who would write the kind of a music that he heard inside himself, somewhat removed from the realities of playing at that time. A performer said about one of his works that it was too hard to play. Beethoven replied, "Do you think I care about your wretched violin when the spirit moves me?" One of the reasons the *Grosse Fuge* sounds like a twentieth-century work is that at certain points there are three different rhythms going on at the same time: two eighth notes, a dotted eighth and a sixteenth, and a triplet. It's not as if one follows the other; they are simply superimposed. It was an astonishing thing to have done in 1827. It points to the simultaneous time screens of Elliott Carter and Morton Feldman. What you're doing with that triplet is squeezing three notes into the time of two. At almost every time point within a measure there is an attack. So it's hard to determine where this note is going to hit. Because it's a three, this is a two, and this implies a four, it's all occurring at the same time. This piece is incessant; it doesn't have a form that you might identify with a work at that time. The *Grosse Fuge* is the only nineteenth-century work that can exist on a wholly modern music concert. It's also the only nineteenth-century work the Arditti String Quartet will play.

Several years ago if you had asked me about the future of the quartet I would have said it didn't have one, that its days were numbered. Most of the quartets I was hearing those days, with perhaps the exception of those of Elliott Carter, were more or less recompositions of the great works of the Second Viennese School. Franz Josef Haydn said somewhere that he could be most shocking when writing for string quartet and that the form enabled him to let his imagination run more freely than in other forms.

String Quartet 1931

Ruth Crawford's *String Quartet 1931* was written in a style best described as dissonant counterpoint. "Dissonant" means unpleasing to the ear. Of course what is consonant and dissonant differs in various periods of history. When the breakdown of tonality and harmony occurred around the turn of the twentieth century with Schoenberg, Webern, and Berg, music freed itself from the reliance on harmony. The consonant intervals (fourths, fifths, thirds, and sixths) began to be replaced by the more dissonant ones (seconds, sevenths, and tritones). Composers who didn't want to base their works on the flow of harmony discovered that if they used enough dissonant intervals, the music would free itself melodically and rhythmically.

Counterpoint occurs when two or more voices or instrumental parts go along relatively independently. Bach's music was contrapuntal; related melodies moved along independently. Much medieval and renaissance music was contrapuntal. With the advent of harmony, Western music became rhythmically less interesting. The flow of the chords became more interesting than the independence of the lines.

Ruth Crawford often uses a technique known as "crabbing" in her works. It simply means turning the melody around and playing it backwards. It's a common technique in contrapuntal music to generate more material and keep the flow of the music going. It's a paradox, that is, in order to move forward you write something backwards. If it is simple enough the listener can hear it. If it's complex enough it remains hidden from the listener. Only the composer knows it's there. The modern term is "retrograde." You can turn material upside down, too. That's called "inversion."

Crawford was interested in verse form and something she called metric form. She thought of musical phrases as sentences, the ends of phrases as rhymes. She thought of music as speech and its structure as syntax.

Ruth Crawford's dissonant counterpoint by itself wouldn't distinguish her quartet from others of the same ilk. It's the third movement that makes this work remarkable. It's a slow movement with sustained tones, often in the form of clusters. The movement starts with the viola playing a low C-sharp. Then the cello, which usually plays the bass line, comes in a semi-tone above the viola. Then the cello moves down to C-natural, a semitone below the C-sharp. So the cello brackets the C-sharp. There's no melody, hardly any rhythm, just long notes. Then the viola moves up to a D-sharp against the C-natural, which is sustained, and then F-sharp, moving up, against an F-natural. The cello weaves above and below the viola. Then the second violin comes in, A-natural, and a B-flat. I'm giving you these roughly. And the cello goes up to a G-sharp while the viola sustains the F-natural. The cello, viola, and the second violin overlap, go above each other, forming clusters. She gives dynamic markings on these long notes, crescendos and decrescendos creating pulses from pianissimo to piano and back again. Everything is soft. As the movement progresses, there are larger ones so that by the climax, the dynamic marking is fortissimo. It was an astonishing movement to appear in 1931. There's a place where the violin holds a note for fourteen measures.

The parts are not hierarchical, the way they often are in other music. I suppose one could say that weaving is a feminine trait, but it also occurs in men's pieces, too. Where it is not experimental is in the climax. It builds up to a climax in a more or less conventional manner, then falls off it, but at about twice the speed. (Actually musicologist Judith Tick discovered that the climax wasn't present in the original but was added seven years later. One has to wonder why Crawford felt compelled to do this.) Then there's a coda (tail), which ends the movement similar to the way it began, except the cello is an octave lower.

String Quartet I/II

Sometime in the Sixties Mauricio Kagel asked me if I knew the Ruth Crawford *String Quartet* and I had to say no. We were never taught it at school. Here was an Argentine composer, living in Germany, who had studied the Crawford *String Quartet*. So in honor of Mauricio Kagel let's look at his *String Quartet I/II*. Written in 1967, this pair of pieces is the only work I know for prepared quartet. Remember how John Cage stuck screws and bolts between the strings of the piano to alter its sound? Well, Kagel inserts knitting needles and paper clips under the strings of the instruments. The work is theatrical, too. The players walk on stage one by one looking behind them, grimacing and sitting in the wrong chair. The cellist sits where the first violinist is supposed to be. Everyone in the audience gets the joke because they know where the first violinist sits. Then, as they play, they stare at each other and smile. It's a kind of theater of the absurd.

String Quartet No. 3

Let's listen to a mystery piece. Let's pretend we're anthropologists and have just landed on another planet. You hear these sounds and have to figure out what the structure is. It sounds like a canon, but what kind of a canon? Each time the theme comes in it is faster than the one preceding it. The canon is in rhythmic proportions 3:4:5:6. The cello plays the motive; the viola enters in a proportion of 4:3; the second violin 5:4; first violin 6:5. The players have to count and be able to come in at those tempos. At a certain point later in the piece everything comes out at the right time. The work is Conlon Nancarrow's *String Quartet No. 3*. Nancarrow's canons are different from Ruth Crawford's, the material is so simple that you can really hear the entrances distinctly. He doesn't disguise them. In the Crawford piece, the canons, inversions, and crabbings are audible but not terribly obvious. They're used more as a means of making the work, the structure is more hidden. Nancarrow's structures are clearer.

Worlds in Collision

For a few years in the early Seventies Bob Ashley wore a leather jacket. Every time he moved there was a crackling sound, the sound of leather. He was a walking sound piece. He might not have thought about why he wore a leather jacket. You heard his presence by a sound that was very identifiable. If you closed your eyes and he walked into a room, you'd know it was he. We were talking once about the future of music and he said he thought it was going to consist of pops and clicks. I loved pops and clicks. Short sounds articulate a space, they can make a space sound in an interesting way, as distinct from long sustained sounds that have kind of a soporific effect. Clicks are so short that you hear what surrounds them, what comes before and after them. Long sounds are continually present, you have to listen to them. Short sounds give the listener short rests; with long tones the listener has to let his or her mind wander in order to get relief. There are political aspects to the duration of sounds.

In the early Seventies, Bob was interested in the works of the science writer Emmanual Velikovsky. One of his ideas was that the universe doesn't necessarily proceed in an orderly manner and that evolution and the geological formation of this planet didn't take millions of years to accomplish. He refutes those ideas by saying that there have been several cataclysmic events that have caused great upheavals on planet earth. In *Worlds in Collision* (1950) he claimed that in historical time, before the biblical Exodus, Venus came perilously close to Earth causing it to tilt slightly, creating the myth that the sun stood still. This and other stories in the Bible were actually natural disasters caused by planetary malfunctions. He claimed to have predicted the temperature of Venus. At the time his books came out, Velikovsky was completely vilified. The astronomical academic community, including Harlow Shapley of Harvard, blackballed him and informed his publisher that they wouldn't buy books, even of other authors, from them. They thought his scientific theories didn't stand up under scientific scrutiny. They thought he was a dangerous crackpot.

Perhaps Bob felt close to Velikovsky because most of us at that period were out of it as far as American musical life was concerned. People thought we were crackpots. If you mentioned any of our names at Princeton, Harvard, or Yale, they'd probably have said so. They don't any more. We thought of ourselves as outside the mainstream. Bob used to say he thought of us as the Satchel Pages of new music. We were just as good as anyone but were kept in the minor leagues. But often it's the crackpot of today who is proven right in the future. A. N. Whitehead wrote a preface to one of Velikovsky's books. He said that every new idea is considered nonsense when it first appears.

Recently there was a festival at the New York Philharmonic entitled "American Eccentrics." It included works of Charles Ives, Henry Cowell, Henry Brant, and Terry Riley. Pauline Oliveros and I were on a panel. Imagine being labeled an eccentric when you simply do what feels natural for you to do in your own hometown. Kyle Gann wrote in the *Village Voice* that Beethoven sometimes used his musical scores for toilet paper. Nobody advertises his *Ninth Symphony* as by a European Eccentric.

String Quartet Describing the Motions of Large Real Bodies

Bob Ashley got the image for his *String Quartet Describing the Motions of Large Real Bodies* from one of Velikovsky's books. If the planet Venus comes perilously close to Earth, it might cause a change in the magnetic field, causing the Earth to tilt, producing enormous cataclysms. I don't know whether this is in the Velikovsky book or not. How would we perceive the planet Venus approaching Earth? Would we know that it's coming? What would we see if a huge object were approaching earth at an enormous speed? I think that got Bob thinking about scale. Something can be so large that you don't see it moving. What if you were an ant and a human foot came down on you, would you see it coming? If something is moving so slowly, you don't see it move, either. You might perceive it at different points along its path, though. Analog becomes digital.

When you slow down a physical movement you see amazing things, the minute movements of muscles and so forth. In 1964, Takehisa Kosugi made a beautiful work, *Anima 7*, during which he took a half an hour to take off his jacket.

In *Quartet Describing the Motions of Large Real Bodies*, the players are asked to draw their bows continuously and slowly, and

STRING QUARTET DESCRIBING THE MOTIONS OF LARGE REAL BODIES

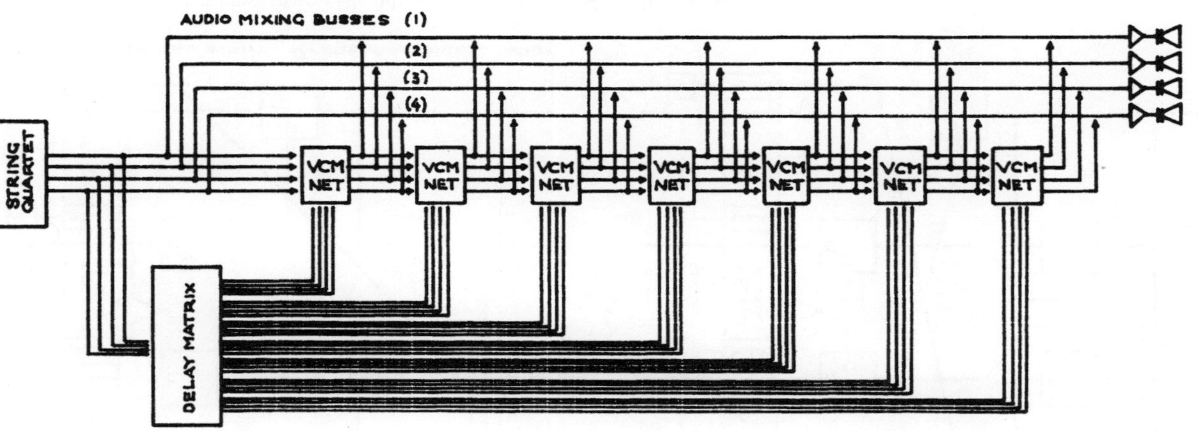

THE BOW IS DRAWN CONTINUOUSLY BUT SO SLOWLY AND WITH SUCH GREAT PREASSURE ON THE STRING THAT THE STRING RESPONDS IN RANDOMLY OCCURRING SINGLE "PULSES." IN THIS MANNER OF PLAYING THERE IS MORE SILENCE THAN SOUND. TYPICALLY, A SINGLE DIRECTION OF THE BOW MAY TAKE 10 MINUTES. INSTRUMENTS SHOULD BE TUNED UNIFORMLY LOW.

USE DIRECTIONAL MICROPHONES EXTREMELY CLOSE (WITHIN 3 INCHES) TO THE SOUND-HOLES OF THE INSTRUMENTS.

THE DELAY MATRIX SHOULD PROVIDE DIFFERENT SIGNAL-DELAY TIMES IN A RANGE BETWEEN 5 MILLISECONDS AND 250 MILLISECONDS FOR EACH OF THE SEVEN GROUPS OF OUTPUTS. DELAY TIME IS THE SAME FOR ALL OUTPUTS IN A GROUP.

WITHIN EACH VOLTAGE-CONTROLLED-MODIFIER NET ANY VC DEVICES MAY BE USED (WITHOUT REGARD TO SYMMETRY.)

USE AT LEAST ONE, OR AS MANY AS SEVEN, VCM NETS, ALTERNATING A-TYPE AND B-TYPE IN SERIES. ALWAYS OBSERVE THE SYMMETRY OF CONTROL-SIGNAL AND PROGRAM-SIGNAL ROUTINGS.

IDEALLY, THE SUM OF THE SIGNALS AT THE LOUDSPEAKERS SHOULD BE NO LOUDER THAN THE UNAMPLIFIED SOUND OF THE STRINGED INSTRUMENTS.

Robert Ashley, String Quartet Describing the Motions of Large Real Bodies, *1972.*

Used by permission of the composer.

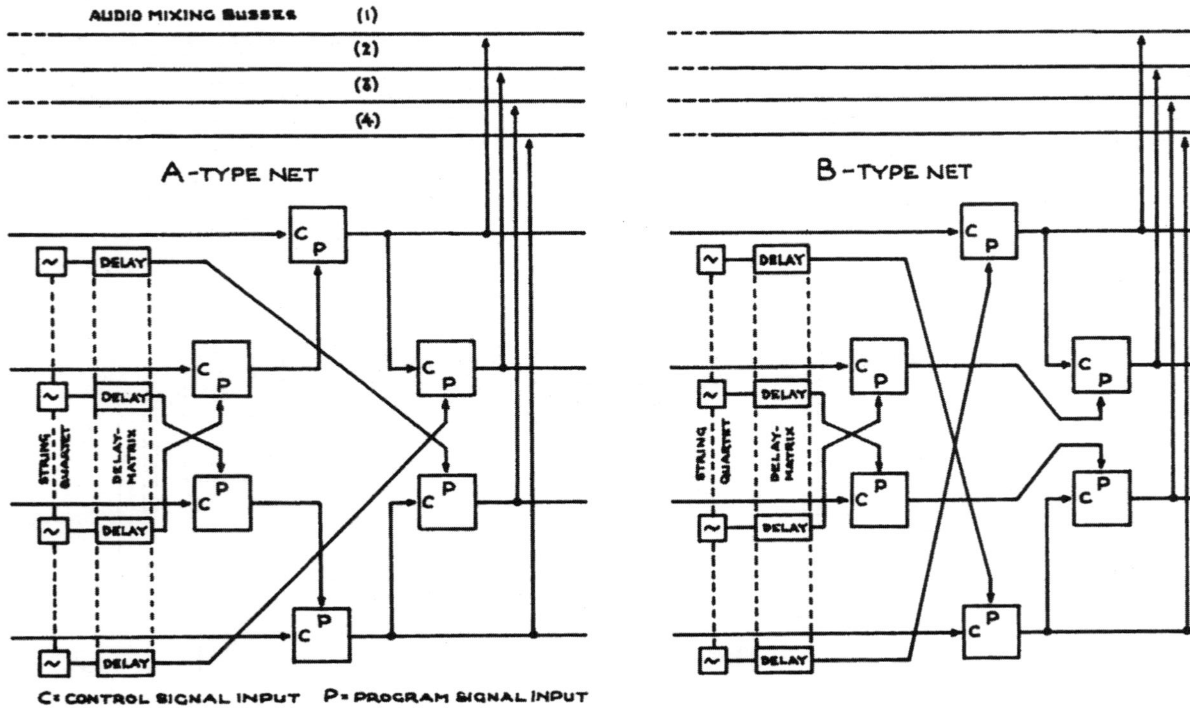

Page 2 of String Quartet Describing the Motions of Large Real Bodies, *1972.*
Used by permission of the composer.

with such great pressure on the string, that it responds in randomly occurring single pulses. A single direction of the bow may take ten minutes. There should be more silence than sound. Normally, a bow length to achieve a smooth sound lasts about ten seconds. A skillful player can extend that to about twenty. Any slower than that, the sound isn't clean.

Bowing may be thought of as an analog phenomenon, that is, a continuous force that causes a continuous result. But by bowing so slowly, the analog becomes digital. The sound consists of a train of separate pulses instead of one continuous sound. It's much like the path of a slowly moving object or one so large that it appears to be slowly moving. Have you ever watched a large airplane landing? It seems to be suspended in air. You don't see its continuous motion; you see it at various discrete points along its glide path.

The score of *Quartet Describing the Motions of Large Real Bodies* is a beautiful visual representation of what the piece looks like in the mind of a composer. The four string players are on the left side of the page, the output, and four loudspeakers, on the right. You can see the sounds of the strings are routed into audio mixing busses and delay matrices. (An audio mixing bus is simply a single channel through which several signals may be sent to a particular destination. Having one fader makes them easier to control.)

String Quartet Score, Front and Back

There are seven VCM (Voltage Control Modifier) nets. Voltage control simply means changing the values of an electronic component by applying a voltage to it. Say you put a sound from a microphone into a filter. By feeding a voltage into the control input, you can drive the filter up and down. Bob uses the term *modifier* to cover a number of unspecified devices. It could include filters, amplifiers, and modulators of different kinds. These were available in the old analog synthesizers. Everything is digital nowadays.

The delay matrix provides delay times between 5 and 250 milliseconds, for each of the seven groups of the output. 250 milliseconds, a quarter of a second, is the longest time delay in the work. In musical terms that's extremely fast, but in electronic terms it's rather long. Use at least one or as many as seven VCM nets alternating type A and B in series. Always observe the symmetry of the control signal and the program signal (the sound of the string). Ideally the processed sounds should be no louder than the original unamplified ones.

The two kinds of nets are different abstract structural ideas. They don't relate to any specific instruments, they're simply Ashley's idea of the routing. We could look at them as pathways. Sounds enter here, get controlled here, go here, and come out here. He's simply designed two ways of how this happens.

The sounds get stored in memory for a certain pre-set length of time. If the delayed sound occurs too soon after the original, you don't hear a time delay, you hear a timbral change. In Fourier analysis a sound wave delayed against itself forms a new sound wave with a different timbre. If the delay is very short, a couple of milliseconds, for example, you don't hear it as a time delay because the sound is still present. You hear its echo inside itself. These rich and beautiful timbres are created not only by time delays but also by voltage control alterations. What's beautiful is that they're all done in such a short time span. Bob was thinking in terms of milliseconds, unheard of in music. First, the players bow extremely slowly, producing pulses of sound, as short as string sounds can possibly be; second, the sounds are routed through voltage control devices and extremely short time delays that change the timbre of the sounds. It's a beautiful chain of events. Much of it sounds almost melodic. That's caused by the resonances of the pulses.

Have you ever thought about what music you'd like to have at your funeral? I'd choose *String Quartet Describing the Motions of Large Real Bodies*. Somebody once said it sounded like the creaking of the rigging of a sailboat. That image brings to my mind the ancient boats they put the Egyptian pharaohs in when they died, to take them to the Western Lands. I have a canoe at home so you could just lay me in it and play Bob's quartet as I float out the mouth of the Connecticut River. (Just kidding.)

Koan

Let's look at James Tenney's *Koan* for violin, written for Malcolm Goldstein. A koan is a Zen term for a question that has no answer. "What is the sound of one hand clapping?" is a koan. Even if there is no answer, you think about the question.

Let's take a look at the family of stringed instruments that are so prominent in Western classical music. They all have four strings. The strings of the violin are tuned a fifth apart—G, D, A, and E; the viola, a larger, alto violin, is tuned a fifth lower—C, G, D, and A; the cello, an octave below that. The double bass's strings are tuned a fourth apart—E, A, D, G—because the instrument is so large, a stretch of a fifth is to much for the player's hand. *Koan* starts with the violinist playing tremolos on the open G and D strings. A tremolo is an oscillation of two notes produced by a fast up and down motion of the bow. (It was used in music as far back as the seventeenth century, to indicate excitement or danger.) Gradually and imperceptibly the player begins raising the bottom pitch. Pretty soon it's a semitone higher, then a whole tone higher, and so on, until finally it reaches unison with the open D string. The two strings are now in unison, that is, sounding the same tone. The violinist continues raising the G-string's pitch until it reaches A, a fifth above the open D. Then the D string is similarly raised until it reaches unison with the A. The process is repeated until it reaches the high E, of the open E-string. It couldn't be simpler. As you listen to Malcolm play it you can hear the grainy sounds of the strings. It doesn't have an aesthetic sheen. There's no vibrato either.

In the Eighties, the From Foundation commissioned Jim to write a quartet. He simply orchestrated the *Koan*. The first violin plays the solo violin part; the rest of the quartet plays long sustained tones. It's the same piece, but slower. Because you have to keep three players together, it is precisely notated. The solo work was freer; the player didn't need to coordinate with anyone else.

I was in Aspen for the first performance. After a few minutes the audience started to get fidgety. I was totally focused on every moment-to-moment sound. I wasn't distracted by contrast. I wasn't waiting for a climax, either. I could hear the small things that were happening in the music. Once you accepted the fact that it wasn't going to change, and there was no story, no climax, you began to hear the acoustical phenomena. Jim's systematic use of symmetry helps you to hear what's going on, too. You don't have to think about contrast, you can focus on the micro-tuning in the string playing.

A well-known composer sitting in front of me was looking around all upset, grimacing and showing the rest of the audience how baffled she was by this work. I became angry because she was interfering with my perception of the music. Her antics were driving me crazy. I wanted to hear Jim's piece! I didn't want to see her acting as though she couldn't understand what was happening. She was acting childish. Then they played a piece by a Pulitzer Prize–winning composer. (Dick Winslow used to call the Pulitzer Prize a "passport to oblivion.") It was a skillful work, it had everything in the book you ever wanted to know about string writing: *pizzicato* (plucked sounds) in all the right places, *col legno*, bowing (sounds made by the wooden part of the bow), sudden *sforzandi*, *pianissimi*, *crescendi*, *diminuendi*, a few thumps here, a couple of plinks there, a little of this, a little of that. There was never a dull moment. The focus changed every few seconds. My mind wandered. The inexorable flow of Jim's piece had me riveted, whereas this one bored me to death.

Thirty Pieces for String Quartet

Let's take a look at one more piece: *Thirty Pieces for String Quartet* (1983) by John Cage. The Arditti Quartet played it on February 27, 1988, in Crowell Hall, a few hours after Cage had given his *Lecture on Anarchy*. Cage had come to Wesleyan for a week of concerts, lectures, and panels organized by Neely Bruce. By *anarchy*, Cage doesn't mean that everybody can fool around or do something self-indulgent. He means that everybody performs the tasks they are given as well as they can, independent of a central authority. We often find ourselves in anarchic situations. We all have our daily work. You have yours, I have mine. We do much of it independently of one another. Cage once said that when you wash your hands you're in an anarchic situation; nobody tells you how to do it. The quartet players were spread out around Crowell Hall. Irvine Arditti (violin) was seated on stage, David Alberman (violin) was on the side steps of the hall, Rohan de Saram (cello) was up in one of the window bays, Levine Andrade (viola) was stationed in the back of the hall. They were spaced far enough apart that they wouldn't be in danger of interacting with each other. Each one was a separate soloist.

Thirty Pieces consists of thirty separate sections, each one lasting a minute. The directions—there is no score—specify three sorts of tuning: tonal, chromatic, and microtonal. The tonal and chromatic parts are written in proportional (spatial) notation, the tonal consisting of sustained, beamed tones, the chromatic part is more virtuostic. In the tonal passages, when a bow cannot be held a full length the player simply stops playing, creating silence, rather than moving the bow in the opposite direction. (Time always moves forward.) The microtonal passages are written in $\frac{4}{4}$, $\frac{5}{4}$, or $\frac{6}{4}$ time. They consist of steady quarter notes interrupt by irregularly placed quarter note rests. This gives a feeling of stability and instability at the same time. It reminds one of the irregular ictus of the percussion part in *Ryoanji*. It's as if Cage wants to make the tuning perfectly clear, which would be hard to hear if the rhythms were as complex as they are in the other two styles. Small arrows coming up from accidentals—sharps, flats, naturals—indicate small deviations in pitch.

Cage pays a lot of attention to extreme bowing techniques, including four kinds of hammered tones (*martellato*): starting with the bow in the air, stopping on the string; starting on the string, ending in the air; starting and ending in the air; and starting and ending on the string. Small pitch inflections are indicated by squiggles. The letter *R* indicates ricochet. All the harmonics in the microtonal sections are upbows. The playing is coordinated only in the sense that each player operates within time brackets. Cage wrote this work for the San Francisco–based Kronos Quartet. He mentions somewhere that he meant its structure to be earthquake-proof.

Cage shows you that while each player plays very specific music, detailed and complex, he or she doesn't do this in relationship to others. There is not the oppression of relating, visual signaling, call, and response. There are just the four related but independent parts. Each player plays very intricate, complex, delicate things, and they're each by themselves, and playing apart from each other gives an extraordinary result, as compared to *Navigations for Strings*, for example, where the four players behave like bees in a hive, or Jim Tenney's monolithic *Koan*, in which there's one system that operates throughout the entire performance. As you sit and listen, you hear a beautiful representation of anarchy. The players are not cutting corners; they're not playing anything they want, hoping nobody will know the difference. They're playing their parts to the best of their ability. Each part is meticulously written, exquisitely detailed. The piece simply ends at the thirty-minute mark. Cages warns against a visual signal to show the ending. It would be too much like having a conductor.

Navigations for Strings

For years I have been walking around hearing or at least imagining those man-made frequencies of the Omega Navigational Network that I encountered in 1980 while recording sferics on a Colorado mountaintop. There were eleven or twelve of them high up in the audible spectrum, around ten to twelve thousand cycles per second. I couldn't get them out of my head. I would sing them under my breath, or whistle them quietly in sort of an idealized form. I compressed them into four tones—B, A, B-flat, A-flat. I don't know why. It's not such a bad melodic cell when you think about it. It's similar to the Bach theme—B-A-C-H, which is used by a lot of composers. The letter "H" in German indicates the note B-flat. Years later Ernst Albrecht Stiebler of the Hessischer Rundfunk (Frankfurt Radio) asked me to write a quartet for the Arditti String Quartet. Without thinking about it much, I simply decided to use these four pitches. I wrote a systematized score, where, over a fifteen-minute period, the four pitches would squash themselves into a single tone between the two middle ones. I can't play it on the piano, because it's in the cracks, midway between the A and the B-flat. I wrote out a number system that gave the lengths of each pitch, based on the four instruments. Instead of the violin playing, as he does in Jim's *Koan*, and then squeezing it down, the four players step or jump up or down to the four tones. The instruments were distributed over the four pitches, and as the piece progressed, the notes were tuned microtonally inward. I purposely gave the players impossible tunings.

A semi-tone can be divided into 100 cents. The human ear can distinguish increments of about twelve cents within that 100. I made gradations of one, or 2½ cents above or below the tones. Impossible to hear. I wanted to give the players a numerical idea of how small the increments would be. I mentioned to Irvine Arditti that the piece was impossible to play. He answered that his quartet was used to playing the impossible; it was the very difficult they found hard to do! So, the G-natural goes up, the B-flat comes down, the G-natural goes up to A-flat, the A-natural goes down in between the A and the A-flat. The score is completely notated, fixed. When the tunings are close you hear audible beating. That's the point of the piece. The goal is not absolute perfection—there's no way the players can achieve these tunings—but to go gradually from the original four pitches to a single pitch, in between you hear the imperfections of the tuning, and you hear the audible beating. The beats are the bumps of sound between the instruments.

Someone asked me once if, in writing for string quartet, I didn't feel as if I were working in an old form. I answered that I didn't feel I was working in an old form; the old form had already been revitalized chiefly by two quartets, the Arditti in Europe and the Kronos in the United States. Because of the great playing of these new quartets many composers now want to write in this form. Another good reason to write for quartet is that you have four dedicated musicians who are used to playing together and rehearsing long hours to perfect their repertoire.

Chronos Kristalla (Time Crystals)
from *The Magic Chord* x 4

La Monte Young composed *Chronos Kristalla* in 1990. It lasts about an hour and a half, not long by Young's standards. It is completely notated. It was written for the Kronos Quartet and they refuse to play music that is indeterminately notated. The material for *Chronos Kristalla* comes directly from *The Magic Chord* section of *The Well-Tuned Piano*. Each player has eight pitches to play, all natural harmonics. Natural harmonics are those tones that are played on the open strings of any string instrument. You simply lightly touch the string at some point along its length to produce a ghostly pure sound. Natural harmonics sound like sine waves, that is, tones with virtually no overtones. That is why La Monte likes them. They have no timbre. Morton Feldman loved harmonics too. They matched the timbre of his piano sounds that were played with a minimum of attack. They sounded like sine-wave tones too. There are artificial harmonics. Artificial harmonics are those that are produced by lightly touching an already stopped string. To help the players, La Monte gives the quartet a Rayna digital synthesizer that is capable of the most exact tunings. Before the concert each player tunes to two harmonics on each string.

Now if you tune your strings in Just Intonation you might assume that the resulting harmonics will also be pure since they will only sound when touched at exactly the right spot on the length of the string. You would think that would insure perfect tuning throughout the performance, but strings are imperfect mechanisms. They stretch and contract a little while being played and are subject to fluctuations in temperature. By the end of Morton Feldman's *Quartet No. 2* the strings are beautifully out of tune. The players, over a five-hour period, have no time to re-tune. The performance takes on a lovely patina of imperfect sound. It's similar to what the aging process does to wine. Unfortunately, on a recording you don't get that; the players have time to re-tune between takes. So even though La Monte hears *Chronos Kristalla* in Just Intonation, in reality it is a little out of tune. But it doesn't really matter; it's beautiful just the same and the intention is there.

AUTHOR'S NOTE

Most of the material in this book was taken from lectures I have given in over forty years of teaching at Wesleyan. I have not attempted to make a complete survey of American experimental music; rather, I have included works I have loved and been personally involved with, either as a performer or friend of the composer. I have not found it necessary to follow each composer's work to the present day. I have included mostly those works as I first encountered them, in the belief that each represents the composer's work as a whole.

This book would not have been possible without the help of over two dozen graduate teaching assistants. I am grateful for their diligence in obtaining scores and recordings from Olin Library, as well as occasionally performing selected works in class. Special thanks go to library assistant Jennifer Thom Hadley and music librarian Alec McLane for expediting last-minute requests from an absentminded professor.

INDEX

ABOUT THE AUTHORS

ALVIN LUCIER is the John Spencer Camp Professor of Music, Emeritus, at Wesleyan University and, with Douglas Simon, the coauthor of *Chambers*. He has been a pioneer in many areas of music composition and performance, including the use of brain waves, room acoustics, and the natural characteristics of sound waves.

ROBERT ASHLEY is a contemporary American composer. He has written some thirty operas for television, one of which, *Perfect Lives*, was featured in Peter Greenaway's documentary *4 American Composers*.